For the Love of RESCUE CATS

Carol Griglione
and Mick McAuliffe

THE GUIDE TO SELECTING, TRAINING, AND CARING FOR YOUR CAT

For the Love of Rescue Cats

CompanionHouse Books™ is an imprint of Fox Chapel Publishers International Ltd.

Project Team
Vice President–Content: Christopher Reggio
Editor: Amy Deputato
Copy Editor: Colleen Dorsey
Design: Mary Ann Kahn
Index: Elizabeth Walker

ISBN 978-1-62008-360-4

Library of Congress Cataloging-in-Publication Data
Names: Griglione, Carol, author. | McAuliffe, Mick, author.
Title: For the love of rescue cats : the guide to selecting, training, and
   caring for your cat / Carol Griglione and Mick McAuliffe.
Description: Mount Joy, PA : Fox Chapel Publishing, [2019] | Includes
   index. | Summary: "This book discusses all aspects of selecting,
   bringing home, and caring for an adopted rescue cat, with a focus on
   shelter cats. Topics include the adoption process, acclimating your new
   cat to her new home, supplies needed, litter-box and behavior training,
   health care, and feeding"-- Provided by publisher.
Identifiers: LCCN 2019031716 (print) | LCCN 2019031717 (ebook) | ISBN
   9781620083604 (paperback) | ISBN 9781607657576 (ebook)
Subjects: LCSH: Cat adoption. | Cats. | Animal shelters. | Cat rescue.
Classification: LCC SF447 .G68 2019 (print) | LCC SF447 (ebook) | DDC
   636.8/0887--dc23
LC record available at https://lccn.loc.gov/2019031716
LC ebook record available at https://lccn.loc.gov/2019031717

Fox Chapel Publishing
903 Square Street
Mount Joy, PA 17552

Fox Chapel Publishers International Ltd.
7 Danefield Road, Selsey (Chichester)
West Sussex PO20 9DA, U.K.

www.facebook.com/companionhousebooks

We are always looking for talented authors. To submit an idea, please send a brief inquiry to acquisitions@foxchapelpublishing.com.

Printed and bound in China
22 21 20 19   2 4 6 8 10 9 7 5 3 1

Contents

DEDICATION

This book is dedicated to all shelter cats everywhere—the ones who are waiting for good homes and the ones who have already found them. To all once-homeless animals, don't give up on humans. Your unconditional love inspires us to strive to do more, not only for you but also for every animal that will follow you. For years, cats have been portrayed as standoffish, aloof, or even "bad luck." Those of us who have loved and worked with cats know that these portrayals are unfair to felines. We wrote this book to help those who love cats and those who we hope will learn to adore them for the wonderful, loving, curious, playful, and sensitive creatures they are.

About the Animal Rescue League of Iowa

Founded in 1926, the Animal Rescue League (ARL) of Iowa, Inc., is Iowa's largest nonprofit animal shelter. The ARL serves animals in need across the state, with a focus on Polk County and central Iowa. The mission of the ARL is to promote animal welfare, encourage and strengthen the human/animal bond, and prevent the overpopulation of pets.

For example, in 2018, the ARL took in more than 11,000 animals from fifty-eight Iowa counties and seven states. Of those animals, 5,857 were cats and kittens, with 3,992 adoptions and 1,364 placed in foster homes. On any given day, the shelter has more than 650 animals in its care at its main facility and four satellite locations. With such a large number of animals to care for and a limited number of full-time staff members for all of its locations, the ARL relies heavily on volunteers to assist in all realms of the organization, from daily care of animals to helping with fundraising efforts. Currently, close to 2,100 volunteers donate countless hours of service.

The ARL is responsible for the care of more than 20,000 animals each year and runs a farm-animal adoption program as well as animal control for the City of Des Moines. The ARL is the only shelter in central Iowa that never turns away an animal in need. This results in a large number of animals and people who depend on the ARL each year. This dependence has grown dramatically since the ARL was founded in 1926.

—Tom Colvin, Chief Executive Officer,
Animal Rescue League of Iowa

Tom Colvin

Tom Colvin has been instrumental in animal protection work in Iowa for close to fifty years. He began his work as a veterinary technician in Waterloo, Iowa; went on to become director of the Black Hawk Humane Society (now called Cedar Bend); and then moved to Des Moines in 1993 to become the ARL's shelter director. He was appointed executive director in 1995 and currently serves as the ARL's chief executive officer. Tom led the initiative to build a new 43,000-square-foot shelter, which was completed in October 2008. Additionally, Tom started a prison program, called Whinny, at Rockwell City Men's Prison, which provides extra care and rehabilitation for neglected horses that come to the ARL until they are ready for adoption.

Tom has been president of the Iowa Federation of Humane Societies since 1981, is a member of the Iowa State University External Stakeholders Advisory Group, and sits on the board of the Iowa Wildlife Center. He has also served on the Iowa Board of Veterinary Medicine. In addition, Tom was a wildlife rehabilitator and has served on Iowa deer task-force committees. He has done extensive work on animal cruelty and puppy mill investigations, working tirelessly on legislation to strengthen Iowa's animal-protection laws, for which he has received awards. Additional successes include legislation that prohibits giving pets as prizes, felony animal-fighting laws, and the 2010 passing of the Puppy Mill Bill.

Programs and Services

- Pet adoptions at four Des Moines-area ARL locations as well as numerous affiliated locations
- Pet behavior counseling and training classes for dogs, cats, and rabbits
- Spay/neuter programs, including Catsnip, PitStop, The Purr Project, The Daily Fix, and Spay the Mother
- Humane education
- Lost & found and ID Me program
- Pet intake of strays and owner-released animals
- Pet first-aid training

CatSnip and Summer Getaway

CatSnip is a no-cost spay/neuter program provided by the Animal Rescue League of Iowa and sponsored by Petsmart Charities. It is provided for anyone who participates in any financial-assistance program and lives in certain zip code areas. Any donations given to CatSnip are put back into the program to provide continued funding for this much-needed service.

The Summer Cat Getaway program gives long-term ARL cats a chance to get out of the shelter during the ARL's busiest time of year and enjoy the home lives they deserve. Approximately fifty new cats arrive each day in the summer, so the Summer Getaway allows the shelter to bring in more cats for adoption.

↑ **Betty is one of the ARL's resident cats and has become quite well known for her regular appearances on the shelter's Facebook page.**

- Cruelty-intervention initiatives
- Disaster planning service for pets
- Whinny program in collaboration with Iowa prison system
- Volunteer opportunities
- Pets in Crisis program, which provides temporary housing for pets of people in crisis (e.g., house fire, domestic abuse, homelessness)
- Temporary Love and Care program for special-needs animals
- Animal-assisted therapy
- Humane euthanasia and cremation services
- Legislation/advocacy for animal-welfare laws
- Contractual relationship with several local governmental entities, including the City of Des Moines, to provide care and all animal-control services to lost and homeless animals found by the public or picked up by ARL animal-control officers
- Horse rescue and adoption program
- Barn Buddy program
- Loyal Friends Club for shelter supporters, which allows them to set up reoccurring monthly donations

HAPPY ENDINGS

Alley

Polk County Animal Control received a call from the local waste-collection company, saying that workers had found a bag of kittens that someone had carelessly put out with their trash. There were six kittens total, but, sadly, only one was alive. The workers who had rescued the kitten gave her a bath before she was picked up by Polk County Animal Control. The kitten, now named "Alley," arrived at the ARL, was nursed back to health in a foster home, and then was placed up for adoption, soon finding a loving home.

Ash

Ash was found by a Good Samaritan who saw her struggling to crawl out of a burning bush pile. He rushed her to the ARL so she could have a chance at survival. The kitten, estimated to be only three weeks old, had burned her ears, paws, and tail but was otherwise doing remarkably well. The medical staff treated her wounds and placed her in foster care with a staff member for around-the-clock care until she recovered from her wounds and was old enough to eat on her own. Her foster mom bottle-fed her every day while her German Shepherd gave the kitten comfort, warmth, and love—the dog even licked Ash's wounds to clean them each day in a true demonstration of compassion.

Ash stayed in her foster home for about eight weeks. Parts of her tail and ears had fallen off due to the burn damage, but she was otherwise a happy, healthy kitty who loved other cats and dogs of all sizes. She was soon placed up for adoption and found a forever family and her very own bed.

1 Choosing the Right Cat or Kitten for You

An Easy Decision?

It seems like a simple decision: You decide you want a feline friend to add to your family. You go to the shelter, you find one you like, and you are done. But it is not that simple, and, quite honestly, it should not be that easy. The cat you choose will be a member of your family for an average of fifteen years. If you decide to add a feline to your family, do it with the intention that it is for the lifetime of the cat—no exceptions.

Cats end up in shelters for a variety of reasons, the most common being litter box or behavior issues. With just a little effort and retraining on the part of you—the owner—you can solve many of these issues. If your cat has behavior issues, be committed to solving them.

What to Consider When Choosing a Cat

Your lifestyle. Are you a homebody, or are you gone much of the time with work and other activities? Do you have other pets? Do you have children at home or plan on having children in the future? Often, people want to adopt a kitten because they believe that the kitten will bond with them better than an adult cat would, but that is just not true. Adult cats absolutely bond with their new families, just as kittens do.

People often choose kittens because they are cute. But, as we all know, kittens grow up to be cats. And if you find that your lifestyle keeps you away from home a lot, a kitten will become lonely and bored; this is when behavior issues start to surface. For someone who is away from home often with a busy lifestyle, a mature cat is the way to go.

With kittens, we encourage people to adopt two at the same time. The kittens will bond with the humans in their lives, as well as with each other. They will keep each other company when their family is away from the house for long hours. At night, when their people are trying to sleep, they will play with each other.

Children. Children are a big consideration when choosing a pet. Consider the ages of your children and their activity level. If your child is five years old and likes to

↑   A child is a great friend for a cat but should not be the pet's primary caretaker.

↑ **An adult cat can adapt to an owner's busy lifestyle if the owner finds adequate time to spend with the cat.**

wrestle and play hard, an eight-week-old kitten probably is not the right pet. A cat that has already been around children is always a good choice.

At the shelter, we often hear potential adopters say, "I told my child that she could get a pet, but she will have to take care of him." That is an unrealistic expectation that often results in the pet being returned to the shelter days, weeks, or months later. It is hard for pets to go in and out of homes. They bond with their humans and, when they find themselves at shelters, they become stressed at being taken away from their homes and the people they love. When we make an "easy-way-out" decision to give up a pet, we are teaching our children that animals can be given away or abandoned at the drop of

Purebred or Mixed Breed?

Many purebred cats find themselves in animal shelters. If you are looking for a specific breed of cat, be sure to check out the cats at your local shelters before looking elsewhere. While animal shelters do get purebred cats on a regular basis, consider adopting a mixed breed cat. Cats, whatever their breed, are fun and curious creatures and can form a bond with the humans in their lives. Whatever type of cat you choose, a cat you adopt from a shelter is sure to give you many years of joy.

a hat. Therefore, if you are considering getting a cat or kitten, go into it fully aware that the adults in the home will be responsible for the majority of the pet's care.

Other pets. You must also consider the other pets in your household when choosing an additional pet. Some people question whether they should even get a cat with a dog already in the home. Cats and dogs can be friends. In fact, they can be great friends. The belief that they are natural enemies has been portrayed in fiction for years, but it just isn't true. While not all cats and dogs will get along, many cats and dogs will form relationships, even sleeping together, grooming each other, and taking care of each other. We have seen this happen at the ARL. Opie, an American Eskimo Dog, and Elmo the cat were brought to the ARL by the same family. When they arrived, the staff took Opie to the dog kennels and Elmo to the cat cages for evaluation. Over the next few days, both were depressed and refused to eat. Opie got to the point where he wouldn't even raise his head when the staff came to feed him. The director suggested taking Elmo to the dog kennels and putting him in with Opie. Instantly, both were happy pets. They slept together and ate together—all was good as long as they were together. The ARL adopted out this dog and cat together as "bonded buddies" to a new home. Such events are not uncommon, and they certainly show the bond that animals can form with each other.

MEWSINGS

Add Another Cat?

Q: Betty called into the Companion Connection radio program one Saturday after hearing us discuss the benefits of adding another cat to a one-cat family. Betty wasn't home much due to her work schedule, and her cat, Boscoe, was alone a lot. At the time, Boscoe was a neutered, five-year-old male and was still playful. Betty was looking for suggestions on finding a good match for Boscoe. She was wondering if she should get a female, as she had heard that two males in the house might be stressful. She was also hoping to get a kitten.

A: Betty should consider getting an adult cat between the ages of two and seven instead of a kitten; sex is not an issue. For cats, it isn't about sex but more about age and personality. Does your current cat want to play all the time, sometimes, or never? Try to find a second cat that matches your resident cat's personality, energy level, and playfulness. Similar personalities will enable the cats to make an easier connection.

Consider the Mix

Amy found a kitten and fell in love. She took the kitten home and named him Hershey. However, Amy already had three Whippets. The Whippets were certain that this new kitten was a toy for them. Being sighthounds, Whippets love to chase and often cause harm to small furry things that run away from them.

For two years, Amy had to keep these pets separated. She gradually introduced them to each other, tethering the dogs to her so they couldn't chase Hershey and cause harm. Gradually, this process worked, and now everyone lives in harmony. The Whippets have learned that Hershey is part of the family.

This is an extreme example of what you need to consider with pets already at home. Are you willing to go to such lengths for however long it takes?

↑ Sighthounds, such as Whippets, have an inherent drive to chase small animals.

Age of the cat. Consider the age of the cat you want to adopt and the ages of the other members of your pet family. People sometimes prepare for the loss of a senior cat by adopting a kitten. The last thing an older cat wants is a young kitten that pesters and bugs him. While the sex of the cat you are adopting isn't an issue, age certainly is. Look at the age and personality of your current cat and get a playmate that will complement her.

Stories about Bonding

For those of you still skeptical about the bonds between animals, let me share a couple of stories involving my own pets. Spirit was a Greyhound/Collie mix and Zorra was a tortoiseshell cat. One day, Zorra was trying to jump up onto the coffee table. She was a little uncoordinated and didn't always complete her jumps. After watching Zorra try three times, Spirit got up and lifted Zorra onto the table with her nose.

Another example of a friendship between a dog and a cat was between Azzurro and his canine housemates. Azzurro, normally an indoor cat, escaped one night when the dogs were let out. Once back inside, the dogs immediately started barking and whining, circling around, and going up to the door. We couldn't figure out why, so we went to see what was going on. When we opened the door, the dogs ran straight outside, directly to where Azzurro was, and began nosing him back toward the door to come inside.

2 What You Should Know about Shelter Cats

We've mentioned that shelters provide a fascinating mix of adoptable cats: purebreds and one-of-a kind mixes in a variety of ages, from kitten to adult to senior. Adopting a cat from a shelter is generally less expensive than buying from a breeder. Adoption also helps reduce the number of cats being bred for profit.

Shelters can provide you with information on the temperaments and personalities of the cats available for adoption because the staff and volunteers handle the cats daily. This helps keep the shelter workers apprised of each cat's condition and also helps maintain the cats' sociability with humans. Some shelters also have cats living together in "cat condos" or "community cat rooms," which allow them to interact with each other. This can be beneficial when they move to new homes that already have cats. For owner-released cats, shelter staff may also have current medical history or pet history from previous guardians. If you are interested in adopting more than one cat, look into the cats that were brought into the shelter together or have become great pals and bonded at the shelter.

Some cats in shelters can be stressed due to a sudden change from the familiar environment of their homes to the unfamiliar shelter environment. They may not be used to cages, and they may miss the "normal" things in their lives as well as their human families. Some of these cats may need extra

Myths about Shelter Cats

People often think that owner-surrendered cats ended up in shelters due to behavior problems, but this is not always true. Pets are surrendered for many different reasons. Many of the cats in shelters have no behavior problems, and the reasons for their surrender have more to do with the owners than with the cats themselves. Furthermore, most behavior problems are fixable, and the issue that brought a particular cat to the shelter may never show up in a new home environment.

patience, assurance, and guidance after adoption. The shelter staff will be able to help you with this transition, but always remember that any cat will need some adjustment time, and your love and patience will pay off.

Socialization

If you adopt a kitten, it's important to encourage her to have good social skills by socializing her as much as possible when she is young. This means having as many people as possible pet, play with, and hold your kitten. You want her to get used to

↑   A good shelter tries to provide comfortable accommodations and enrichment
     opportunities for the cats.

being handled by as many people as possible, which includes being picked up, brushed, and petted by people other than her own humans. One great way to do this is to have friends and family visit, especially right after you get your kitten. Provide toys, such as ping-pong balls, cat fishing-pole toys, or paper bags, so people can play with your kitten. See chapter 7 for more games and enrichment activities for kittens and cats of all ages.

As your kitten continues to grow, you should continue to handle her often, at different times, and for different lengths of time. Also, have people touch your kitten's tail, ears, and paws so she is accustomed to being handled all over. You want your kitten or cat to be social and to want to be with humans. At the very least, she should never put her teeth on you, even in play.

DID YOU KNOW?

At many shelters, all cats are spayed/neutered, microchipped, dewormed, and vaccinated before they are adopted.

Behavior through the Ages

Acquaint yourself with the various general social and behavioral traits of cats throughout their lives so you know what to expect no matter the age of your newly adopted cat.

Reward Good Behavior

Like all animals, cats learn through association. If the cat is rewarded for a behavior (whether by her human or by a self-rewarding behavior, such as scratching), she is more likely to repeat that same behavior (desirable or undesirable) in the future. To get rid of an undesirable behavior, you will need to teach your cat a positive alternative behavior; for example, scratching a post instead of the sofa. By rewarding the post-scratching with high-value rewards, such as favorite treats, the sofa-scratching will fade away. Be careful to not unintentionally reward actions that might seem fun or cute at first but will become problematic. Remember, the more we reward appropriate behavior, the better behaved our cats will be.

Three to Eight Weeks

What to expect: A kitten's social play begins and increases steadily. She starts to use the litter box, play with objects, and explore climbing, running, scratching, and predatory behavior.

What you should do: Introduce your kitten to frequent, gentle handling and play with various people, including men, women, and supervised children. Take kitten socialization classes, if available in your area. Reward your kitten's appropriate friendly behavior toward humans and all other animals using treats and play. (*Note:* Always use toys to play with your kitten. Never use your hands and feet because this teaches your kitten bad habits.) Provide litter boxes with low sides for easy entry. Be sure to provide toys and scratching posts. Teach your kitten to go into a carrier.

Nine to Sixteen Weeks

What to expect: At this stage, your kitten continues to learn social skills. A kitten's social play peaks during this time, and you will see her more vigorously exploring the environment and climbing.

What you should do: Continue socializing your kitten. If she has not had previous social education, initiate it slowly. Kittens that have not had adequate experiences during early socialization may not have good social skills and may require extra effort to acquire them. Your kitten may need a larger litter box at this age. Provide vertical space and climbing structures.

Seventeen Weeks to One Year

What to expect: Social play will decrease. A kitten is more likely to be subordinate to larger adults, but she may also challenge these cats for status.

What you should do: Provide food puzzles and food toys. Be sure to continue to play with your cat and reward friendly behavior. You may want to reevaluate the size of the litter box again as well.

↑

DID YOU KNOW?

If you notice any behavior changes in a cat of any age, consult your veterinarian to determine whether medical issues could be contributing to the behavior issues. If the cat is healthy, consult a veterinary behaviorist or an animal behavior specialist. Behavior problems are best treated early.

One to Six Years

What to expect: Your cat may start to slow down during this time frame, so watch for weight gain. If your cat gains weight, check with your veterinarian before changing her diet. Your cat will mature socially approximately between two to three years of age; her personality can be strongly affected by genetics and early life experiences.

What you should do: Continue to play with your cat and reward friendly behavior. Provide your cat with enriching and entertaining activities.

Seven Years and Older

What to expect: Changes in appetite can occur. A decreased activity level may lead to decreased social interaction with you or other animals. The occurrence of medical problems can increase with age.

What you should do: Continue to play and interact with your cat. Your cat may not be as active or interactive as she once was, but this still is important. Monitor her appetite and water intake, and contact your veterinarian if you notice increases or decreases.

The Five Freedoms

The welfare of animals encompasses both physical and mental well-being. The Five Freedoms are a set of internationally recognized animal-welfare standards that outline what responsible owners and animal-welfare organizations must provide. They were first set forth by the Farm Animal Welfare Council and then adopted by many other organizations. We must do these things to keep our pets happy and healthy.

1. **Freedom from hunger and thirst by ready access to fresh water and a diet to maintain health and vigor.** This means that every animal must always have access to clean, fresh water. Provide your pet with a sufficient amount of nutritious food to help keep her in good health and at a healthy weight.

2. **Freedom from discomfort by providing an appropriate environment, including shelter and a comfortable resting area.** Giving your pet adequate shelter is very important. For cats, most of which live indoors, owners must provide warm, comfortable places to live.

3. **Freedom from pain, injury, or disease by prevention through rapid diagnosis and treatment.** Know the signs of illness in your cat. The number-one sign of illness is the animal acting lethargic, tired, or sluggish. Another way to help your cat is to keep her environment clean and free of any hazards that might cause injury.

4. **Freedom to express normal behavior by providing sufficient space, proper facilities, and company of the animal's own kind.** It's easy to know your pet's normal behavior when you spend a lot of time with her and give her a lot of attention. But just like people, animals can become bored and lonely. Provide your cat with a cat tree to climb or access to a window where she can watch the birds. Toys are also a great way to keep your cat mentally stimulated.

5. **Freedom from fear and distress by ensuring conditions and treatment [that] avoid mental suffering.** All animals deserve to be happy, so give your cat a lot of love. Also avoid conditions that introduce unnecessary anxiety and stress to give your cat freedom from mental suffering. Remember, you mean the world to your cat, so always strive to make her feel as special as she makes you feel.

3 Bonds of Love

Human-Animal Bonds

Being involved with an animal shelter for as long as I have been, I have heard thousands of stories of the special relationships that humans experience with animals. I never tire of these stories. They confirm that there are countless people everywhere who truly love their animals. These stories also tell me that the connections we have with our animals can fulfill our lives.

It makes sense. Pets are with us through it all—marriages, divorces, moves, losing jobs, getting new jobs, and deaths in our families. They spend all the major moments of our lives with us. They listen. They never judge. After a hard day at work, a cat owner comes home to a house where the cat runs to the door and meows a hello. Our cats don't care what we look like or what kind of mood we're in. They are just happy that we are with them. We are their whole world.

Those of you who have experienced unique bonds with animals have already discovered this special relationship. For those of you who are just bringing animals into your homes for the first time, I want to share a few of my own stories.

First, there was my dog Freida. She came into the ARL at a mere two weeks of age after her mother had been hit by a car. Freida came home with me so I could foster her until she was old enough to be adopted. But after bottle feeding and spending all my free time with her, we were bonded like I could never have imagined. Of course, I adopted her, and we spent the full sixteen years of her life

together. When my mother died, I remember holding Freida and whispering to her. She licked my tears, asking nothing of me. I knew that as long as I had her with me, I would be OK. Freida has since passed away, but I think of her and the warm memories of the relationship we had every day.

Sometimes, a connection can be immediate. Over my years at the shelter, I have probably met hundreds of thousands of animals. While the staff and volunteers love them all, each of us connects on a deeper level with only a handful.

When I started volunteering at the shelter, I walked dogs and spent very little time with the cats (which is completely different now, of course!)—until one day, when a certain cat caught my eye. I spent the next week not being able to get that cat out of my mind. The next week, I adopted him—my very first cat—and my life changed. Azzurro and I had connected from the minute we looked at each other.

When I moved the first time, this special bond really became apparent to me. Azzurro spent the first two nights in our new home literally sleeping on top of my head (he typically never slept on the bed). It was like he had to know I was there to be OK in this new place. The same thing happened when we moved a second and third time as well. Just as humans turn to animals for comfort, animals take comfort in their human families.

Animal-Animal Bonds

While we talk about human bonds with our animal friends, it is just as important to mention the bonds that form between animals. At the shelter, we have witnessed this bond between animals too many times to count. What is particularly fascinating is that bonds exist between pets of different species that have lived together. For example, a guinea pig and a cockatiel came into the shelter together from a family that didn't want them anymore. They were so bonded that the bird wouldn't eat unless he could see the guinea pig.

Another such pair was a rabbit and a guinea pig. Observing how they cared for each other and the way the rabbit, Violet, protected her guinea pig friend, Teapot, was truly amazing. Any time someone approached their living quarters, Violet would step in front of Teapot—not for attention, but as if to check the person out first. Once she decided that the person was OK, she would step aside and allow the person to pet Teapot.

Otis the cat and Sam the dog were another bonded pair. As is typical at a shelter, when someone brings a dog and cat in together, the different species go to separate housing areas. With Otis and Sam, the staff noticed that, when they were apart, neither one would eat or do anything other than lie around. When we realized the situation, we moved them together into a dog kennel, and all was fine.

↑ **It was love at first sight for Azzurro and Carol.**

↑ **Cats who live together often form strong friendships.**

The experiences of witnessing these bonds between animals led to a policy change at the ARL. Recognizing how pets of the same or different species bond, the shelter keeps the bonds intact through its Bonded Buddy adoption program. When a bonded pair of pets—same species or not—is brought in together to the shelter, the pair must be adopted together, and adoptive owners must sign an agreement stating that they will keep the pets together.

Daily, my own animals demonstrate their bonds. My cats rub on each other; they wash each other's faces and ears. One of my cats must be in close proximity to another one, or he throws a meowing fit. Perhaps one of the strongest examples of bonding I have seen was between two of my horses, Satch and Rio. Satch was clearly the leader of my small herd of three, but before Charlie came into our lives, it was only Rio and Satch. Rio and Satch loved to play together with orange construction cones. One horse would toss it up in the air and the other would go get it, toss it, and so on.

The two horses were once separated for a week when Rio had to be in the equine veterinary hospital for a sprain. When Rio came home, he needed a couple weeks of stall rest. The day we brought him home, we set him up in his stall and then came out an hour later to check on him. Lo and behold, there in his stall was an orange construction cone. My husband thought it was a great idea that I had put it there, while I thought he had put it there. We soon discovered that it was Satch who had dropped it there! Over the next few days, we observed Satch getting the cone and bringing it to Rio.

I recently saw a car magnet that read "Who Rescued Who?" It really struck a chord. We say we that we "rescued" or "saved" our adopted pets, but when I think about it, that is only half the story. These animals all rescue us in one way or another. I am just one of the lucky ones who received the gift of realizing what amazing creatures we are blessed to walk with on earth. My message to all potential adopters is "find your bond."

↘ **With proper introductions and supervision, unlikely pairs can become best friends.**

4 Bringing Your New Cat Home

Once you have decided to add a cat or kitten to your family, you need to make sure everyone in the household is prepared for the new pet and is ready to contribute to her care. Telling your children that you will get them a cat if they take care of her is neither responsible nor in the best interest of the cat or the children. Adding a pet to the family needs to be a decision to which everyone in the family is committed. The cat you bring home is depending on it.

Decide, or at least discuss, who will feed and water the cat and who will clean the litter box. Additionally, having some knowledge about cats and their behavior is important. You need to know when the cat is playing and when the cat is scared. You need to know what behavior indicates that your cat is not feeling well and should visit the veterinarian. You need to know how to act and interact with your cat depending on her behavior. You should find, as most people do, that after living with your cat for a while, you are able to read the cat's behavior.

Supplies for Your Cat

Have the supplies you need for your cat or kitten ready before you get her or get the necessary supplies when you adopt her. Some animal shelters, including the ARL, have pet-supply stores inside the shelters. You will need the following items to care for your cat, keep her safe, and make sure she feels at home:

- Collar
- Food and water bowls

- Food
- Litter box and scoop (see Chapter 6)
- Litter (see Chapter 6)
- Toys (see Chapter 7)
- Brush or comb
- Scratching post
- Bed
- Nail clippers

Identification for Your Cat

Be sure to have proper and secure identification on your cat. Even if your cat lives indoors all the time, there could be a moment when she slips out the door. Your cat needs a collar and identification tag as well as an implanted microchip. Some animal shelters already microchip at the time of adoption; if not, it is a simple procedure that your veterinarian can do. Even if your cat is microchipped, she still needs an identification tag with your name and phone number in case you need to be reached. An identification tag is also good if your cat has to stay at the vet's office or a boarding facility overnight.

The type of collar you get is important. We recommend a "safety" or "breakaway" collar. These collars, if caught on something, will open and allow your cat to escape. This is important both inside and out, if your cat should get caught on a curtain rod or tree limb, for example. (See the Cats and Collars on page 181.)

Acclimating Your Cat

It is interesting to observe your cat come out of her cat carrier when you first bring her home. Does she bolt out of the carrier, anxious to check things out, or does she run under the nearest couch, bed, or dresser? A scared, hesitant cat will need more time to acclimate to a new environment. Be sure to be patient and give her lots of love and time to adjust. A bolder cat will still need reassurance, love, and attention but is going to acclimate to her new home in a shorter period of time. Remember, every cat is different.

Have the litter box set up before you bring your new cat or kitten home, and show her where it is located soon after you arrive. If you have adopted a kitten, put her in the litter box so she can feel the litter. If you have an adult cat, just showing her the box is enough. (See Litter Training in Chapter 6.)

If you do not have other pets, allow your cat to explore. (If you have other cats or dogs, refer to Introducing a New Cat to Other Pets later in this chapter.) With a kitten, you may want to limit where she can go. You do not want her to wander too far from the litter box and forget where it is when she needs it.

Spend time with your cat as she is exploring to supervise her and keep her safe. Before you brought her home, you should have "cat-proofed" your home by putting away cleaning products, human medications, and other household chemicals. You do not want your cat

↑ **A collar and ID tag are essential accessories for your cat.**

to get into these containers or even lick the outside of the containers, in case some of the liquid has dripped. Secure electrical cords to baseboards and put caps on outlets. Keep pens and pencils in drawers. Rubber bands and hair ties can also be hazardous if ingested by your cat or kitten, so put them out of her reach.

As you accompany your cat on her explorations, be proactive in looking for dangers that you may not have previously considered: a cat could fall into an open toilet, chew on a toxic plant, or eat foods left out on countertops. Look for items lying around that she might chew on or swallow, like toilet paper, tissues, and paper towels.

Cats need their own space, too. As we've mentioned, it is always a good idea when bringing a new cat home to set up an area or room that is hers and includes her food and water bowls, a litter box, and her bed. Do not place these items next to each other; arrange her bowls, bed, and litter box in different areas of the room. Your cat's area should be in a low-traffic room that kids and other pets don't frequent. This will be your cat's safe space to sniff, eat, scratch, and play while she gets her bearings. Scatter her toys around. You can even clear off a windowsill for her and have soft music playing. She will appreciate the chance to feel out her new family from inside her haven.

Give your cat time alone in her room or area to get comfortable before you come in to play with her. Then, visit her often and let her out to explore and run around (see Chapter 4 if you have other pets in the home). With a whole new life in store for her, your cat will need some time and space to check out her surroundings and all her new playthings.

Remember that cats like structure. Keep to a routine with your pet during her first few days and weeks. Leave the litter box where you initially put it unless you absolutely have to move it. Feed the same food and use the same litter so the scent and feel on your cat's paws are the same. If you need to make changes, try to wait until a little later, after you have established a bond and relationship with your cat.

Visit the veterinarian within the first few days of bringing your cat home. This is important so that the vet can get a baseline of your pet's health right away. Most shelters will provide you with health documentation on your cat that you can share with your veterinarian to make him aware of your cat's history in

↑　**Facilitate and supervise your new cat's introductions to young family members.**

↑　**Kittens and cats love to explore, and countertops are a favorite.**

terms of vaccination, spaying/neutering, microchipping, and any health problems or treatments given before adoption. You may want to make this veterinary appointment even before you bring your kitten home. Maintain veterinary records for the life of your cat and be sure to provide your pet with regular veterinary medical care, which is a necessity for good health.

Feeding Your New Cat

"How do I feed my new cat or kitten?" is a common question among new cat owners. You may wonder what to feed, how much to feed, and how often to feed your cat. Cats have different needs, so having a conversation with your veterinarian about your cat's dietary needs is important. When you adopt a cat, ask the shelter what your cat has been eating. Most shelters use donated food, so your cat may not have eaten the same food all the time and, thus, have a varied diet. However, if your cat is used to eating a certain type of food, and you are changing your cat's diet, you will want to gradually switch to the new food by giving her a mixture of the old food and the new food. Lessen the amount of old food and increase the amount of new food every few days until the cat is eating only the new food. This gradual change will decrease the likelihood of diarrhea.

Whether you feed your cat dry, canned, or semi-moist food, be sure to purchase a high-quality product recommended by your veterinarian so you are sure that your cat is receiving an adequate supply of vitamins and minerals. Do not add any vitamin or mineral supplements without a veterinarian's approval; excess supplementation may actually harm your cat.

Most cats are comfortable with what we call "free feeding," which means that food is left out and available to them at all times. However, if you have an overweight cat or a cat with specific medical needs, you may need to feed a more restricted diet, including scheduled feedings at specific times during the day.

Kids and Cats

Anyone who has grown up with a cat or kitten knows what a great experience it is. Your cat can be your kids' best friend after a tough day at school or while going through a teenage heartbreak. Likewise, bringing a new cat or kitten home is an exciting experience, especially for kids. It is important to make sure that your children, no matter their ages, know how to handle their pet in a humane and compassionate manner. Following are some tips for fostering a great relationship between kids and cats.

Teach children how to handle a cat properly. Show the kids that to pick up a cat, you support the cat's hindquarters in one hand and use the other to support her

↑   **Children must be respectful of and gentle with the cat.**

chest. Hold the cat gently and securely, close to your body. Never pick up a cat by the scruff of the neck. Never allow kids to pull the cat's tail or whiskers or poke at her. If your kids are too young to responsibly pick up the cat, do not allow them to pick her up. Instead, show them how to pet her gently and slowly.

Supervise kids and cats. Supervision is especially important with a new pet. Teach children to respect the cat and do not allow them to chase or corner her, even in play. The cat may bite if she feels threatened. Encourage calm, nonthreatening interactions. If your kids cannot be calm and gentle, allow the cat an escape route into another room. For example, put a baby gate across a doorway with 6 inches (15 cm) open underneath so the cat can get under the gate but the kids don't have access to the room. Or provide a cat tree where the cat can get up high, out of the children's reach.

Do not allow children to disturb a sleeping or eating cat. Also give the cat some space when she is using her litter box. Tell your children that when the cat is sleeping, eating, or using her litter box, they should not bother the cat.

Do not allow rough play. Rough play encourages your cat to use her teeth and claws on you. Play with your cat using cat toys that you have bought or made. For example, many cats love to play with (or in!) a simple paper bag. Toys such as ping-pong balls or soft toys that your kids can toss for the cat to chase are great. (See Cat Toys and How to Use Them in Chapter 7.)

Do not allow children to tease the cat. Teach kids the difference between teasing and playing.

Teach children how important it is to keep your cat indoors. Help children understand the importance of keeping their pet safe. Teach them to watch the cat when the door is open so she does not accidentally run out the door. We strongly caution against letting your cat outdoors. However, if you do, a safety collar, ID tag, and microchip may be what brings your cat home if she goes missing.

Share the responsibility of caring for your cat with your children. Never expect your children to assume all responsibility for a pet.

Teach the kids to treat the cat as a member of the family. If there are issues with your cat, seek help from a cat behavior specialist. Your child will learn that you don't give up on a family member—instead, you work things out.

Introducing Your New Cat to Other Pets

Introducing your new cat or kitten to a cat, a dog, or another pet (or multiple pets) already in the home can be tricky, but it is one of the most important things to do

↑ **Bring the cat, in her carrier, into the area you've designated for her.**

correctly when bringing home a new feline family member. Don't just let your pets meet and sort it out on their own; things could go very wrong. Even if neither of them gets hurt, they probably will never get along.

Other Cats

Begin by bringing your new cat into your home in a cat carrier. Many shelters will provide you with a cardboard carrier when you adopt a pet; otherwise, bring your own cat carrier for your new cat. Immediately confine the newcomer to one room with a litter box, food, and bed, and keep the cat separated from the other cat(s) in the home for a few days. The biggest mistake you can make in building relationships between your resident cat and a newcomer is to let the newcomer roam through the house right after coming home. Patience is an absolute necessity in building a lasting relationship between the cats.

Visit your new cat, play with her, pet her, feed her, and make her feel that this is now her home. Remember that your new cat is probably confused and frightened. You need to reassure her that all is well. Leaving a TV or radio on will give your new cat some background noise and help her feel comfortable.

Scent is critical to getting cats used to each other. While your new cat is still separated from the resident cat, take a bath towel and rub it on your new cat as if you are trying to dry her off. Then, take the same towel and rub it on the resident cat. You are taking the scent of your new cat and putting it on the resident cat. Leave that towel somewhere around the house where your resident cat hangs out. Take a second towel and repeat the procedure, but this time begin with your resident cat. Leave that towel in the room with your newcomer cat.

By doing this exercise every day, you are exposing the cats to each other's scents. When they finally meet face to face, they will smell familiar.

You can enhance the procedure by dabbing vanilla extract on the base of each cat's tail, where they can smell and lick it. This cements the scent issue, making the cats smell like the same scent—vanilla. Do this every other day.

After a time, switch the cats. Put your resident cat in the room where you had sequestered the newcomer, and let the newcomer out into the rest of the house. The newcomer can explore his new surroundings and spread his scent around the house. This is another way to allow both animals to get used to the scent of the other before actual face-to-face contact. This process may take a few hours or a few days, depending on how the cats react. Start with a couple of areas in the home and then switch the cats back to their original locations. Repeat the procedure the next day.

↑ **Mealtime can be a good time for the first face-to-face meeting.**

After a few days, it is time for an introduction. Do this when you are going to be home. Do not leave the cats together unsupervised after the initial introduction. Open the door to the sequestered room and allow the new cat to come out on his own and explore. Allow the cats to meet each other on their own terms.

You can also use a baby gate across the door of the sequestered room and allow the cats to meet with the baby gate between them for the first few times. This is a good idea when you are uncertain about how the introduction will go.

If you feed meals at a set time of the day, mealtime is a good time for face-to-face introductions. The cats will be so busy eating that they won't have time for fighting. Be sure to give each cat her own bowl on opposite sides of the room. Make it a special dinner, with great-smelling food.

However you decide to approach the introductions, do not force a meeting between your cats, as this may cause unnecessary fighting. Let them get acquainted gradually to help develop a positive relationship and lessen the chances of any territorial issues. Expect hissing, spitting, and growling, but do

→ **Use a towel to acquaint the resident cat with the new cat's scent, and vice versa.**

↑ **Safely leashed, these buddies enjoy walks together.**

not interfere unless an actual fight breaks out. If this happens, throw a blanket over each cat and confine them to different quarters. Keep them separated until they have calmed down. Then start over.

To encourage a good relationship between the cats, reward them when they are in the same room or area and behaving appropriately. They don't need to love each other from day one, but they do need to be able to be in the same room without warfare. If they are in the same room, and there are no behavior problems, give them treats and tell them "good kitties" in a soft voice. You can also take a fishing-pole toy and play with them together, as this will be a fun activity for both of them.

Another great technique for cat introductions is to use toys. After keeping the cats separated as previously described, let the new cat out of her room and immediately dangle a fishing-pole toy so that the cat is interested in the toy. When your resident cat comes out to meet the new cat, keep dangling the toy so that she is interested in the toy as well. Continue to dangle the toy so that they (hopefully) both begin to play or at least stay interested in the toy and not focused on each other.

You could also use ping-pong balls to toss in front of the cats so they chase after them. This lets both cats see that the other is playful and nonthreatening. Offer them treats while they are playing with the balls. Make their first meeting fun with play and treats so they will associate those good things with each other as well. These techniques not only help introduce the cats but also help them start to form a bond.

The Family Dog

When bringing a new cat into a household with a dog, you must make the introduction a positive experience for all involved. The process is similar to introducing a new cat to a resident cat; it is best to have a slow introduction with gradual exposure to each other. When the time comes for the cat and dog to meet, it should be done slowly and in a controlled situation. When you allow the cat to roam, your dog must not be allowed to chase or harass the cat. Having your dog on leash ensures that your cat is safe, and you can teach your dog how you would like him to behave around the cat.

The most important thing is to teach your dog to stay calm and reward him for doing so. In doing this, your dog will also learn that when the cat is present, he gets treats, which will build the dog's positive association with the cat. When you feel that your dog understands how you want him to act, let the dog greet the cat slowly. Leave the dog on leash in case you have to grab him in a hurry. Make sure that your cat has places where she can escape and get up high to feel safe, especially if your dog tries to chase her.

Rewarding your cat when the dog is present works, too. Determine what your new cat likes in the way of treats and play. When the cat is near the dog, reward her with her favorite treat or play a favorite game.

Your Pet Bird

An important factor to remember when introducing your new cat to the family bird is genetic makeup. Your cat is genetically predetermined to be a predator, and the bird prey. With that in mind, placement of the bird's cage will depend on the type of bird and cage setup. Small or hanging bird cages should be placed away from any objects that the cat could use to jump onto the cage. All perches should be placed in the middle of the cage so that the bird can sit on the perch, and the cat cannot make contact with the bird. Do not allow your cat to stalk or harass your bird. You may want to create a hiding place in the cage where your bird can feel safe. You can also place a skirt around the bottom portion of the cage to block the cat's view of the bird.

DID YOU KNOW?

You should never leave your new cat alone with a resident pet unless you are 100 percent sure that nothing will happen.

Pretty Mama and Kittens

We found four kittens, Gus, Fiona, Ziggy, and Delia, in a nest in the bushes on a Friday afternoon outside our publishing office. We didn't know if they had been abandoned or if their mother was a feral cat in hiding. I called my vet and the ARL, who told me not to leave the kittens outside. The kittens seemed healthy, their eyes were open, and they were very mobile. I volunteered to take them home over the weekend and feed them every three hours as instructed. On Monday, I took them to my vet, who determined that the kittens were three and a half weeks old, weighing 10 to 12 ounces (0.3 kg) each, and gave me advice on their care and feeding.

Determined to raise them to good health and find them homes, I took them back to the office, where I would continue their care. Within an hour of returning to work with four little kittens, my vet called to tell me that they had a mother cat at the clinic who was nursing four kittens. He told me to bring my four kittens back to see if this mother cat would accept and nurse them, too.

↑   Gus and Fiona

Pretty Mama was laid on a table and presented with the four tiny kittens. With barely a sound, she let the kittens nurse immediately. The vet offered to let the kittens stay with Pretty Mama. The kittens flourished, nursed and cared for by a mother cat, which is always the best way to raise kittens.

↑   Pretty Mama

Five weeks later, after the kittens were weaned and spayed/neutered, they all needed homes. We kept two, Gus and Fiona, at the office. I found a home for the other two, Ziggy and Delia, with my neighbor, Jean. Pretty Mama went home with my friend Carol. Veterinary staff and clients adopted Mama's four kittens. In all, Pretty Mama and eight kittens found happy forever homes.

—Sue

↑   Ziggy and Delia

5 Choosing a Veterinarian

Having a veterinarian for your furry family member(s) is as important as having a good medical doctor for the humans in the household. It is important to establish a good relationship with a veterinarian who you like and trust for your cat. Ask friends for recommendations or ask the shelter where you adopted your cat if there are any veterinarians volunteering their time or services at the shelter. Make appointments to meet with several veterinarians, just as you would with any other doctor. Choose a vet with whom you are comfortable and who will answer your questions.

Be sure to observe the goings-on of the office itself when you visit. Observe the demeanor of the office staff and those working with the animal patients. Do you feel that they are kind and compassionate? Would you want them handling your cat? You want to be comfortable with all aspects of the veterinary clinic.

First Visit to the Veterinarian

The shelter from which you adopt your cat should provide you with a health record that lists all vaccinations given and other health-related information that you and your vet will need; this could include any tests run (such as for feline leukemia virus and feline immunodeficiency virus), nutrition, parasite control, microchipping, spaying or neutering, and grooming. Sometimes, however, the shelter doesn't know much about the cat's health history and can provide you with only limited, if any, information. If you have other cats at home, and

especially if the newcomer's health history is unknown, keep the new cat separated from your other cats until your vet has had a chance to examine her.

Take your new cat to your chosen vet as soon as possible and bring any health records with you. In addition to giving the cat a general physical examination and testing for the previously mentioned diseases, your vet will also likely test a fecal sample for the presence of intestinal parasites. Even if your new cat has had previous stool samples analyzed, it is important to keep in mind they are only snapshots in time of parasite life cycles, and one sample may not reveal all parasites. Having repeat fecal exams is important, especially with a kitten. Intestinal parasites deprive the infected cat of important nutrition, causing weakness and susceptibility to viral or bacterial infections. Keeping your cat parasite-free is important for her long-term health.

During your cat's physical examination, your vet will also check for external parasites, such as fleas, ticks, and mites. External parasites cause many common skin disorders and can transmit other diseases, such as Lyme disease. Your vet can provide effective treatments and control methods to get rid of and/or prevent external parasites.

Upper respiratory-tract viruses are extremely common in cats, so you may see one in your newly adopted shelter cat. Symptoms are similar to those of a head cold. Most shelters deal with hundreds of cats, and, just like with children in a classroom, colds spread easily. Most common respiratory viruses will run their course with little treatment as long as a secondary bacterial infection does not cause complications. Make sure an infected cat is hydrated, eating well, and has a place to rest. Other viruses may require more extensive treatment under the guidance of your vet.

Emergency Care

We hope that you will never need emergency care, but it is important to know what to do if your cat needs urgent after-hours health care. Ask your veterinarian for an emergency-care plan and a recommendation for a twenty-four-hour veterinary facility in your area. Program the emergency clinic's phone number into your cell phone and keep the phone number and address on your refrigerator (or somewhere else handy).

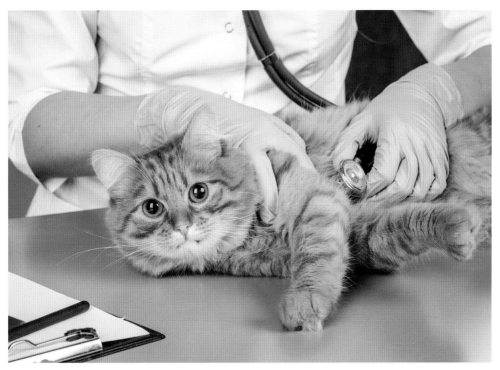

↑ The vet will check your cat's heart and lungs as part of her regular physical examination.

During your cat's first visit, your vet can give you advice on your cat's nutrition, which contributes to her overall health. Your vet will also discuss the importance of yearly physical examinations to assess your cat's overall health.

Vaccinations

A series of vaccines for kittens and regularly scheduled booster vaccines for adult cats are one of the best ways to protect your cat from deadly infectious feline diseases. We recommend feline distemper (feline panleukopenia) and feline leukemia vaccinations for all cats because these illnesses are the most common feline diseases. They often prove deadly to cats of all ages but are especially dangerous for kittens. Your kitten should begin to receive vaccines against these diseases at approximately six weeks of age, once the protective maternal antibodies from her mother's milk have begun to lose their efficacy. Additionally, the rabies vaccination, which is given at eight to twelve weeks of age, is required by law in

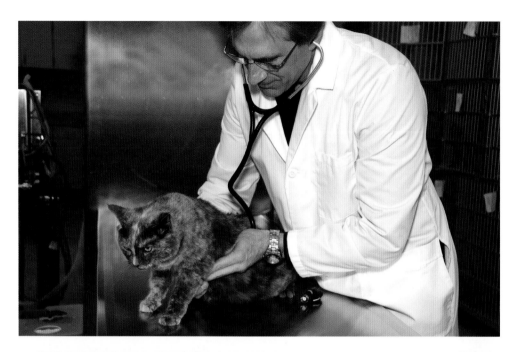

↑ A thorough look at the skin and fur should reveal the presence of external parasites.

DID YOU KNOW?

Not all intestinal parasites are visible to the naked eye. However, an owner may see an intestinal parasite that resembles a white threadlike worm (roundworm) or grain of rice (tapeworm) in the cat's stool or near the cat's tail. These worms are treatable with medication that you can get from your veterinarian. After treatment, have your vet examine a fecal sample to ensure that the parasites have been eliminated.

most places in the United States. If you adopt an adult cat and are unsure of her vaccination history, you will need to get your cat vaccinated as if she were a kitten to ensure effective protection. Following the initial vaccination series, your growing or adult cat will require a set of booster vaccinations every one to three years, depending on the vaccine type. These additional vaccinations are necessary to keep your pet's immune system ready to fight off disease.

The most common combination vaccine, usually called FVRCP, protects your cat against three diseases: feline distemper, feline viral rhinotracheitis, and diseases

Which Vaccines?

How do you know which vaccinations your kitten or cat should receive? Ask your veterinarian. If you ask other pet owners or search the Internet, you'll find different answers to the questions of which vaccines your cat should get and how frequently she should get them. This is yet another reason why you should have a veterinarian whom you trust.

Considerations include:

– The likelihood of your cat contracting the disease, including risk factors such as where you live, your cat's diet, and other cats in the area

– The severity of the disease

– The overall success rate versus side effects of the vaccine

– Your cat's health and disease history

↑ **Vaccination protocols can vary based on where you live and the risk of individual diseases.**

caused by feline calicivirus. Feline distemper (panleukopenia) is a highly contagious and deadly viral disease in cats. Generally, the first FVRCP vaccination is given when your cat is six to eight weeks old. The vaccine is then repeated at three- to four-week intervals until the kitten is sixteen weeks old. After this initial vaccination series, boosters are given one year later and then every three years, to keep the cat protected. An adult cat that is adopted without a health history would receive two vaccination boosters three to four weeks apart. The initial vaccination series should be boosted one year later and then every three years, according to the American Association of Feline Practitioners guidelines. Keep proper records of your cat's vaccinations and speak with your vet if you have any questions or concerns.

Vaccines may produce some mild negative side effects, such as inflammation around the spot of injection, lethargy, loss of appetite, and fever. Rarely, a cat may experience a severe reaction to a vaccination in the form of a lump or swelling around the injection site that does not go away within a few days. Contact your vet immediately, as this may be a sign of a severe and potentially life-threatening reaction to the vaccination.

HAPPY ENDINGS

Sugar and Spice

I adopted two three-month-old kittens from ARL West. They made themselves at home and learned the rules very quickly. Sugar (tiger) is absolutely fearless and started playing with our rescue dog, Merry, right away. Spice (calico) is a little more cautious, but she also got used to Merry. Both kittens love to snuggle.

—Rebecca

Carmella and Ziggy

When I went to the ARL fashion show event, I was a little worried that I would want to bring home another small dog; I already had a Miniature Dachshund. However, the big longhaired cats really caught my eye. I thought seriously about adopting a Ragdoll cat, but Carmella's coloring was just so pretty. I couldn't bear the thought that Ziggy and Carmella might have a hard time finding a home because they needed to stay together. I decided that I had plenty of room in my house and my heart for two cats.

It is ironic that I initially chose Carmella because she was so pretty, when Ziggy is the one who has really stolen our hearts. Carmella was a bit reserved and shy at first, although not skittish or fearful, and she became more outgoing once she settled in. Ziggy, however, lives to eat and be petted. Strangers are all just friends he hasn't yet met. He spends his nights alternating between my bed and my daughter's. Whoever he can wake up to give him a good scratch behind the ears gets the pleasure of his company.

Carmella and Ziggy are both great cats. I have a feeling that I will eventually turn into the little old lady in a rocker with Carmella on my lap in front of the fire while Ziggy, Katie (my daughter), and Roxie (my dog) rule the rest of the house.

—Marce

6 Litter Training

With any luck at all, the mother cat has given your new kitten some sound litter-box training. Even though a kitten is more energetic than an older cat, she is not as rigidly set in her ways and will be more open to litter training. An untrained older cat might require a little more patience on your part.

Choosing the Right Litter Box

Choosing the correct litter box for your cat is important. If you adopt a cat from a shelter, the staff will be able to provide some insight as to what kind of litter box—covered, uncovered, liners, no liners—they have been using as well as the type of litter.

You also need to consider the size of your cat. A litter box that is too small may cause issues, and your cat will stop using it. Your cat should be able to easily get in the box, use it, and turn around to cover up her waste. If you adopt a kitten, you can start with a small box, but remember to upgrade as the cat grows to a larger litter box of the same texture and design that the cat is used to.

While some cats use covered litter boxes for years without any problems, they can be a common source of litter-box issues. If possible, use an open box with no cover. If you are unsure, you may want to provide a covered and an uncovered litter box and see which one your cat prefers.

As your cat ages, you may need to change litter-box styles. If the cat has always used a covered litter pan, a change in body composition or mobility may make

removing the cover important. If a cat has become overweight, she may no longer fit comfortably in a covered box. Likewise, an older cat with musculoskeletal changes, such as arthritis, may find an uncovered box or a litter box with lower sides much easier to use.

Type and Depth of Litter

The choice of litter material is important. Some cats prefer a plain clay litter without any added odor control. Other cats may prefer fine clay litter that clumps and allows frequent and easy litter-box cleaning. It is best to use the same type of litter that was being used at the shelter because your cat is already accustomed to it.

Generally, most cats prefer a depth of at least 2 inches (5 cm) of litter. This depth gives a cat enough litter to cover up her waste and then go back to use the litter box later in the day before you've had the chance to clean the box with a scoop. Your cat will let you know if you don't get it right!

We recommend clay or clumping litter, but to see which type of litter your cat is most likely to use, place a box with clumping/scoopable litter next to a box with another type of litter.

Setting Up the Litter Box

As you set up the litter box, find a spot where you are comfortable leaving the box for an extended period of time. Moving the box from place to place can cause a cat, and especially a kitten, confusion as to where she is supposed to be going. The location should be easily accessible and offer your cat privacy; for example, do not place your cat's litter box in a high-traffic area or near the noisy washing machine. You also do not want to place it in a dark hallway or closet area. The litter box should be set up so the cat can use it and then "escape" the area quickly if she chooses. If there are multiple cats in the home, you may need multiple litter boxes in several locations. Cat people speculate that cats do not share space equally and some may be unwilling to go to

↑ **An uncovered litter box with a scoop.**

→ **Make sure that a covered litter box is easy for your cat to enter and exit.**

Introducing the Litter Box

Show your adult cat the litter box but do not put him in it. If you have a kitten, place her in the box so she can feel the litter.

certain locations to use the litter box. Make sure you have more than one litter box if you have a multilevel house. Kittens are like children and sometimes the urge to go hits them without warning, so it is important for them to have easy access to a box.

Litter-Box Maintenance

For some cats, it is necessary to keep the litter box scrupulously clean. This may mean changing the litter daily or at least removing feces every day. You should scoop the litter box at least daily and clean it completely twice a week. Even if you use clumping litter, clean the box out completely and wash it with hot, soapy water. A cat may be reluctant to use the litter box if it has recently been deodorized or if the cat dislikes the odor of the cleaning products, so rinse the box well after cleaning. Do not use bleach to clean the litter box because the smell is just too strong.

100-percent whole-kernel corn litter

Clay litter (comes with or without odor control)

Corn fiber and baking soda litter

Covered Litter Boxes

A covered box may hold in odors associated with infrequent cleaning, which will cause the cat not to use it. Removing the cover usually solves the problem. There is also an issue that we call "escape route syndrome," which is sometimes common in cats living in households with other cats, other pets, kids, or a lot of activity. In such a situation, a cat can develop a fear of going into a covered box and not being able to see what is coming from one direction or another. The cat can only see one escape route—the door of the covered box—which can make her feel trapped inside the litter box, so she chooses not to use it. Removing the cover will immediately solve this problem.

Dealing with House-Soiling

Inappropriate elimination is the most common behavioral complaint of kitten and cat owners. Inappropriate elimination can include urine or stool deposited outside the litter box as well as marking behaviors, such as spraying or horizontal urination. You can solve these types of undesirable behaviors fairly easily if you are willing to make some small changes.

A cat can also experience defecation problems. After your vet has ruled out medical problems as the cause, you'll have to look at other possible causes. In many cases of inappropriate urination or defecation, behavior modification or adjustments to the

DID YOU KNOW?

Litters with perfumes or other additives may cause your cat to rebel against using the litter box. Some cats have an aversion to these scents.

cat's environment can help. Defecation problems are typically easier and faster to solve than urination problems, but both can be solved.

Medical Reasons for House Soiling

- Urinary-tract diseases
- Stones or crystals in the bladder, bacterial infections, and certain idiopathic inflammatory diseases of the bladder and urinary tract, which can cause pain and an increased urgency to urinate

- Kidney and liver diseases, which can cause the cat to drink more and urinate more frequently
- Age-related decline in brain function
- Endocrine disorders, such as hyperthyroidism and diabetes
- Decreased mobility and sensory function
- Nerve, muscle, or joint problems, which can lead to discomfort, stiffness, or weakness that prohibits the cat from climbing into the litter box or getting into a comfortable position for elimination

↗ **Choose a location that gives your cat some privacy but doesn't make her feel trapped.**

→ **Keep it clean! A cat will avoid using a dirty litter box.**

Litter-Box Liners

Some cats don't mind liners in their litter boxes. Others absolutely hate them and will refuse to use litter boxes with liners. Experiment to see if your cat is bothered by a liner in her box. Make sure that the liner is fixed in place so your cat doesn't get caught in it.

- Discomfort or difficulty in passing stools, poor bowel control, or an increased frequency of defecation (colitis, constipation, and anal sac diseases fall into this category)

Non-Medical Reasons for House-Soiling
- Type of litter or litter box
- Location of litter box
- Type of flooring (substrate) under the litter box
- Frustration, stress, or anxiety
- Marking

Problems and Solutions

It is important to note that most cats will never have litter box problems. If your cat is among the small percentage that do, you will likely be able to work with her to get her back in the box successfully—it will just take some adjustments and some patience. Too many cats are turned into animal shelters each year due to "litter box issues" that were solvable.

Problem: Litter box location
Solution: For a cat that shows a clear location preference for her accidents, placing a litter box in the location where she eliminates may help. If the cat uses the box in that location, leave it there for one week. Then, you can slowly move the box to your desired location with a setup similar to the place where the cat was inappropriately eliminating. Do this slowly and carefully to ensure that

DID YOU KNOW?

Cleaning the litter box too often, especially if you are dealing with a kitten, may set up the cat's expectations that, as an adult, her litter box will be cleaned after every use. Likewise, a cat may refuse to use a litter box that is not cleaned often enough.

Possible Reasons for Not Using the Litter Box

- Medical problems
- Location of litter box (or frequently moving the litter box)
- Unclean litter box
- Litter type
- Litter box size

- Privacy issues
- Number of cats compared to number of litter boxes
- Other pets or activity in litter box area or territory

If your cat isn't using the litter box, and nothing is working, get help as soon as possible. Visit your veterinarian to make sure there is not a medical condition. Once your kitten or cat has been cleared medically, consult your veterinarian or an experienced behavior specialist who uses only positive behavior-modification techniques.

the cat follows the litter box and continues to eliminate in the box as you move it. It is important to move the box only 6 to 12 inches (15 to 30 cm) at a time and leave it in the new location for at least one day. When moving the box from one room to another, or up or down stairs, you can cover longer distances as the cat continues to follow and use the box.

Problem: Substrate preference
Solution: If your cat is having accidents on a particular type of surface, such as carpeting or tiled floors, it may indicate a substrate preference. If the accidents happen in only one or two places, do not allow the cat to be unsupervised in those locations, and make sure that you always know where the cat is when you are home. You can accomplish this by putting a bell on your cat's safety collar. In some cases, you can permanently prevent access to the problem area by closing doors, putting up barricades, or confining the cat away from the area.

↑ **A kitten does not automatically know to use a litter box but should figure it out fairly quickly.**

Another tactic is to make the surface's texture less appealing. Remove carpeting or make any surface uncomfortable with double-sided tape or a plastic runner with the nubs facing up. You can also reduce the appeal of the surface by eliminating all odors that might attract the cat back to the area; give it a thorough cleaning with an odor-neutralizing product.

Problem: Type of litter
Solution: Changing the type of litter may make the litter box more appealing to the cat. For a cat that prefers to eliminate on only one type of substrate, such as a wood floor or carpet, offer other litter choices. For a cat that prefers solid or hard surfaces, an empty litter box or one with minimal litter might work. Some cats may prefer clumping litter, cedar shavings, or recycled newspaper. A carpeted ledge around the litter box or some discarded or shredded carpet can help increase the appeal for a cat that prefers to eliminate on carpets. Potting soil or a mixture of sand and soil may be preferable for a cat that eliminates in plants or soil. It may require a little imagination and a few tries to determine what your cat prefers. Your choice should be based on the

A Gradual Change

If your cat was using her litter box and then you decided to change the litter to something "better," you may now have a problem. If for some reason you change litters, make the change gradually. Mix some of the new litter in with the old and, over a period of time, increase the ratio of new litter to old litter until you've completely switched over.

type of surfaces in the home on which the cat is eliminating.

Problems Persist—What Next?

Once in a while, even after making the litter area more appealing and decreasing the appeal of the soiled areas, the inappropriate elimination continues. Confining your cat to an area away from the previously soiled areas is often necessary to reestablish litter box use. We recommend a small room, such as a laundry room, extra bathroom, or bedroom where the cat has not previously soiled. In this area, make sure that the litter box and litter area are appealing, with no deterrents to using the litter box or surfaces on which the cat is likely to soil. Also give your cat bedding, food, and water in this area.

Most cats will require confinement for one to four weeks. The longer the problem has existed, the longer you will need to confine your cat to establish good litter use. Confinement, however, may not be required all the time. For example, if the cat only eliminates outside the litter box at night, or in the morning when you are getting ready for work, then this is the only time when you need to confine your cat.

Many cats will not eliminate in inappropriate areas when supervised. If this is the case with your cat, you can let her out when you are available to supervise. It may also be possible to allow your cat out of confinement with minimal supervision for the first few hours after she has eliminated in the

→   If you have more than one cat, you should have more than one litter box.

↑ **Temporary confinement can help reestablish good litter box habits.**

litter box. Allowing some time out of confinement and giving some food treats immediately following elimination in the litter box may serve to reward litter-box use. Over time, a cat that has been confined should be given more freedom and less supervision.

Keep in mind that confinement will not necessarily solve the problem long-term if you do not address why your cat quit using the litter box in the first place. For lasting success, you need to solve the problem of why your cat stopped using his litter box so he can live out and about your house as a member of the family.

Using Drugs to Treat Elimination Problems

While we recommend only drug-free behavior modification, drug therapy can be helpful when stress, anxiety, marking, or a medical component is involved. However, if the cat's behavior is due to a substrate preference, location preference, or any type of aversion, drug therapy is unlikely to be helpful. You

DID YOU KNOW?

In rare cases in which the cat will not use the litter box at all, you may need to confine her in a cage with a floor pan covered in litter and a ledge for perching and sleeping to get her to use the litter again.

will need an accurate diagnosis to determine if such therapy will be helpful, and your veterinarian will prescribe the drug that he or she feels is most appropriate.

Commonly used drugs include buspirone, antidepressants, and benzodiazepines. You can medicate your cat, and the problem may subside for a period of time, but unless you figure out what is causing your cat to avoid using the litter box, the problem will resurface. All drugs have the potential for side effects, some of which can be serious. Drugs can also change your cat's personality. The best thing to do is work to solve the environmental and behavioral problems without drugs.

What *Not* to Do

- Do *not* react out of anger. Your cat is trying to communicate that there is a problem, so never punish your cat for not using the litter box. If you punish your cat when she doesn't use her litter box, you are adding to the stress she is already feeling. Instead of stopping the problem, you may have just exacerbated it. Only use positive methods to solve a litter-box problem.
- Never rub a cat's nose in her accident. This is not going to solve the problem; it will only make matters worse. In addition, this is completely unhealthy for your cat.
- Never physically place your cat into the litter box with

→ The litter texture can play a role in whether the cat uses the litter box.

To establish regular litter-box usage and discourage inappropriate elimination, focus on modifying the environment and the cat's behavior.

- Preventive measures or deterrents to keep the cat from returning to soiled areas.
- Litter trials, using two or more litter types.
- Location trials, using two or more litter-box locations.
- Litter-box trials, using two or more styles of litter box.

the idea that you are signaling her to use the box. In actuality, this can cause the cat to think that she is not supposed to relieve herself in the box and instead that it is a place where she gets punished.

- Do not use a squirt bottle. It is difficult to use a squirt bottle without being seen by your cat. If your cat sees you squirting her, she could become afraid of you.

- Never take an indoor cat and put her outside to live because of a litter-box problem. Indoor cats are indoor cats and should stay that way. You need to work to solve the litter-box problem for your cat.
- Do not consider drug therapy unless you have first explored all other options and modifications with a behavior expert. Using drugs in partnership with your veterinarian is only a last resort.

Dealing with Spraying

Spraying is separate from litter-box issues; instead, it is usually a territory-related behavior. When cats spray, they do it in a horizontal or vertical position. Horizontal spraying means that the cat squats as if urinating normally but does it outside the

box. It is easy to mistake horizontal spraying for regular inappropriate urination. However, the modification for a spraying cat is quite different than that for a cat that is not using the litter box. Vertical spraying means that the cat backs up to a wall and sprays urine on the wall. Vertical spraying needs to be addressed from a behavioral standpoint.

We see an increase in cat behavior calls relating to spraying during the spring and summer months. This makes sense because people tend to let their cats out to roam the neighborhood when the weather is nice. Your indoor cat sees these trespassers on his property and sprays.

To address spraying issues, you must first find out if it is an outdoor or indoor territory issue. Is there a stray cat outside the house, or is there a new pet in the home or not enough bathroom and feeding areas?

The first priority is to make sure that your cat is spayed or neutered. The majority of spayed or neutered cats will not spray, so if your cat is spraying and has not been altered, take care of that matter right away.

Spraying Cats

Determine if the spraying problem is an inside or outside territory issue and then try the following solutions:

– Feliway® is a synthetic cat pheromone that comes in spray or plug-in form. It is not a drug, so it will not have any long-term effects on your cat. It tends to relieve stress in cats and can be useful if the spraying issue is focused inside your home.

– If you discover an outdoor cat coming to your house and potentially causing the spraying issue, talk to the owners of the visiting cat. Ask them to keep their cat inside.

– If the visitor is a stray, work with the local animal control unit or shelter about humanely live-trapping the stray and getting her to a shelter for care, or consider a Trap-Neuter-Return (TNR) Program. See page 152.

– Close curtains or blinds so your cat cannot see the outside cat.

– Use outside environmental deterrents, such as turning on your lawn sprinkler at the times of day when the cat is coming to your yard. See Chapter 14.

↓ Outdoor cats spray to mark their territory.

Which Cat Is the Culprit?

Q: I have multiple cats. One of them is not using the litter box. How can I tell which one is soiling?

A: Confinement of one or more of the cats may be necessary to discover which one is not using the litter box. You can also set up a camera to record video of the litter-box area to assess the situation. Another method is to add a safe fluorescent dye to each cat's food, one cat at a time, that will cause the cat's urine to glow when examined under a black light—this will determine which cat is the culprit.

Thinking Outside the Box

Q: My cat, Teddy, has started to defecate outside the litter box. Teddy has always used his litter box. I have started using clumpable litter. Could that be the problem?

A: It could have been the change from clay litter to clumpable litter. However, as I probed further, I discovered that Teddy's owner had switched to clumpable litter so she wouldn't have to clean the box except to scoop out the clumps. Once she began cleaning the box thoroughly at least once a week, Teddy was back to using the litter box right away, regardless of the type of litter.

House-Soiling: Determining the Behavioral Cause

First, your cat needs a complete physical examination, urinalysis, and, in some cases, additional diagnostic testing to either diagnose or rule out medical problems that could be contributing to the cat's elimination problems. Some problems may be transient or recurrent, so your vet may need to repeat some tests to diagnose the problem. If you've either ruled out or treated all medical problems, and the house-soiling persists, you will need to establish your cat's comprehensive behavioral history, including the following information, to establish a diagnosis and modification plan:

- Information about the home environment
- Type of litter box and litter used
- Litter-box placement and maintenance
- Previous litter-box training
- Cat's litter-box use versus inappropriate elimination
- Onset, frequency, duration, and progression of problem elimination
- Location of inappropriate elimination, including types of surface, horizontal or vertical surfaces, and whether it is urine, stool, or both

- New pets in the household
- Other household changes that might have occurred around the time the problem began
- Patterns of inappropriate elimination, such as time of day, particular days of the week, or seasonal variations
- Relationships between the soiling cat and people/other animals in the home

UTI Infections

Q: I took my cat, Pumpkin, to the veterinarian when she started having litter-box issues. She had a urinary tract infection (UTI), which cleared up with medication. However, for some reason, Pumpkin still won't use her litter box. She is a five-year-old spayed female and had never had a UTI before.

A: Pumpkin had started to associate the burning and tingling of her UTI with the litter box because when she was using the litter box to urinate, the infection caused her pain. Thus, she started thinking that the litter box was the source of the pain. To get Pumpkin back into the litter box, the owner needed to change the box so that Pumpkin recognized it as a new box. Then, when she used it, she didn't have the same pain because the UTI had cleared up.

You can have similar results by changing either the size of the box or the type of litter. I suggest putting a second box with a different type of litter (I only recommend clumpable or clay) near the old box. So, if the old box had clumpable litter in it, use clay in the new box, or vice versa. Let your cat see you setting up the new box with the new litter. Curiosity will get her into the new box, and because she doesn't experience the pain of the infection, she will feel differently about this new box. She will think that everything is fine and will start using the new box.

A Stable Location

Q: I just adopted Stephen, an eight-week-old kitten, and I'm already in love with him. I'm not sure what to do because he's peeing in the living room instead of in his litter box.

A: As I talked more with the owner, I found out that she had been unable to decide where to put the litter box and had moved it eleven times in the course of twenty-four hours. She assumed that the kitten would just know where the box was and would use it.

Kittens are like little children. They can't "hold it" for long periods of time while they are hunting for the litter box, so you must leave the box in one spot.

Monster in the Basement

Q: My five-year-old cat, Baxter, has always used the litter box in the basement until recently. Now, every morning—and only in the morning—Baxter urinates at the top of the basement stairs.

A: A home visit showed that Baxter's litter box was right next to the hot water heater. Every morning, when the family was getting ready for work and taking showers, the hot water heater made loud clanging noises. Baxter was scared to go to the basement to use his box when there was a "monster" right next to it. We moved the litter box across the basement and, because the water heater was old and needed to be replaced, Baxter's owners got a new one. Baxter was quickly back to using his box. Most cats know to use their boxes, and they want to. But in Baxter's case, fear kept him from it. We need to think in their terms, not ours.

Scary Area

Q: I caught a stray feral cat and her kittens in a live trap. They are in my basement in a big kennel. My two indoor cats, Lucy and Gracie, refuse to use their litter boxes or food bowls in the basement. Lucy and Gracie have both started urinating and defecating outside their box as well as upstairs. How can I get Lucy and Gracie back to the basement to use their boxes and to eat?

A: I explained that as far as Lucy and Gracie were concerned, there was a "monster" in the basement—the monster being the wild cat and her kittens. Until that cat and her kittens weren't in the basement anymore, it was unlikely that Lucy and Gracie would be going down there. Their owner needed to put litter boxes and a feeding station upstairs.

While Lucy and Gracie's owner was doing a good thing by caring for this mother cat and her kittens, she needed to remember that she still had to accommodate her indoor cats. After moving the litter and feeding stations upstairs, Lucy and Gracie were back to using their boxes right away and eating normally. Lucy and Gracie knew to use the box, but they were not willing to go to the now-scary area to do it.

7 Toys and Enrichment for Cats

Cat Toys and How to Use Them

Toys are an important component in keeping your cat happy. Choosing the right toys and using them in the right way are equally important. There are hundreds of types of cat toys on the market. It can be difficult to determine which ones are best for your cat and her happiness and emotional growth.

Safety is a factor when choosing toys for your cat. The old saying "curiosity killed the cat" can be true. Items that are most attractive to cats can be the most dangerous. String, yarn, ribbon, paper clips, and rubber bands can all be ingested and cause serious health issues or even death for your cat.

Keep your eyes open for dangerous items that may interest your cat. Remove them or move them to an area or container your cat cannot get into. Check labels on stuffed animals. If the item is safe for children under three years old, then the stuffing and parts will likely be safe for your cat.

Cats tend to like soft toys that they can carry around. Rigid toys aren't appealing to them and most likely will be ignored. Cats also have personal preferences as to which toys they favor. The age, size, and activity level of your cat will play key parts in making decisions about her toys. Furthermore, especially in the days of technology, you need to consider the environment your pet lives in and which toys will be fun, exciting, and safe. Whatever toys you offer your cat, remember that they should be fun for her and not create stress or frustration.

Be Interactive

On average, your domestic cat will sleep for about twenty hours each day. Today's cats are not as active as their ancestors because they no longer have to hunt for their food or travel long distances to find new hunting grounds and water. Domestic cats don't have a great deal of energy throughout the day, other than maybe to find a comfortable sleeping spot by the window.

The occasional cat will play on her own or with other cats in the house, but it's likely that you'll need to either be a part of playtime by using interactive toys or find an enticing toy that your cat will play with on her own.

Toys for Active Play

Ping-pong balls are a favorite for active cats. They are lightweight, and they bounce and roll easily. Cats love to bat at them, and they are too large to be ingested. If you have dogs in the home, keep in mind that they may be able to crack, break, and swallow the balls or the fragments.

For fun, put several of the balls in a dry bathtub. Show your cat the toys and let her bounce the balls around for hours of enjoyment. Just remember to remove the balls at bedtime, or you will hear them bouncing around in the middle of the night.

Sisal-wrapped toys are fun for your cat, and she may like to carry them around the house. Some cats prefer sisal to soft toys.

Fishing pole toys are great for playing with your cat. You can sit and watch television and play with your cat at the same time. You should always be sure to let your cat catch the "prize" at the end of the pole, so she feels that her hunting skills are working. Play with your cat, let her catch it, and then play some more. This will keep your cat from becoming bored and frustrated. Plus, it makes her feel good.

Empty cardboard rolls from paper towels or toilet paper are fun for many cats. Make them even more fun by unrolling a little of the cardboard to get them started on playtime. Plastic round shower curtain rings can be batted around

→ **Cats can make toys out of almost anything!**

as singles, or you can link several together and hang them from a doorknob. Your cat may also enjoy a cardboard box that she can jump into, lie down in, and hide inside.

Toys for Comfort

Sometimes a cat wants comfort rather than active play from her toys. Cardboard boxes can also be comfort toys for your cat. If using a box for comfort instead of play, make sure the box is big enough for your cat to get inside and lie down.

Stuffed animals are favorites. Provide stuffed toys that are small enough to carry around or lie on. If you have a cat that wants to hunt the toy and "kill" it, make sure that the toy is about the same size as your cat. Toys with parts such as legs or tails are even more fun and attractive to cats.

Toys to Avoid

Avoid offering your cat certain types of toys. For example, do not let your fingers and toes be used as toys. Such play can encourage biting behavior to develop. Similarly, toys that are like gloves or otherwise fit onto your hands can also cause play-biting behavior to develop. Stay away from these types of toys to avoid problems later.

Catnip can become an issue for some cats. When some cats play with catnip toys or eat catnip, they relax and have fun. For others, however, catnip can affect personality in a negative way. They get overstimulated, which can increase play biting or other undesirable behaviors.

↑ Engage your kitten in a game with a ping-pong or other small ball.

← Add to the fun of a favorite toy by playing with your cat.

MEWSINGS

Simple Toys

Q: Are there simple items around the house to use for cat toys? I have two cats, and I don't want to spend a lot of money on toys.

A: One of the best toys is a paper (not plastic!) bag or a cardboard box. Cats will play with them for hours and sometimes even sleep in them. Put them out for play for a couple of days and then put them out of sight for a week or two. Bring them back out, and they will be like new toys for your cat.

Getting the Most from Toys

Provide your cat with toys, use the toys with her, and encourage your cat to have fun with them. These suggestions may help:

- Rotate your cat's selection of toys weekly, making only a few toys available at a time, but keep them out and easily accessible. If your cat has a favorite toy, such as a stuffed mouse or soft toy for cuddling, leave it out all the time. You don't want to rotate the comfort toys, just the play toys.
- When rotating the toys, be sure to always provide one that allows your cat to "hunt," one for your cat to baby, one for her to carry around, and one for her to play with and bat around.
- Use caution with laser lights. Use them sparingly, as a lot of cats become overstimulated by the rapid movement. When this happens, even when you stop, the cat will obsessively keep looking for the light, which is not good for her emotionally.

Enrichment for Cats

The goal of enrichment is to provide your cat with variety during her days and nights. Enrichment should reduce stress as well as introduce change into a stagnant environment. An environment that doesn't change could become boring and create stress. Things used to improve your cat's life should be easy to physically move, easy to clean, and be safe and fun for your cat.

↑ **A stuffed toy can provide a little comfort and companionship.**

Cats need more to do than lie around and sleep all day. They need toys and diversions that will stimulate and enrich their lives, just like humans do. Think of things that will stimulate your cat's senses of sight, sound, smell, and touch, but don't try to cover all of the senses at once. You don't want to give your cat sensory overload!

Anything you do to enrich your cat's world should be done gradually so she doesn't become confused or stressed. For example, if you were playing a new video game and had to start at the most difficult level, you might try it once and never want to touch it again because it was too hard from the start.

There are four areas of your cat's life in which you can provide enrichment: environmental, social, training, and natural.

Environmental Enrichment
Feeding

Rather than providing food in a bowl, try stuffing food into a Kitty Kong® or treat ball. Or put food inside an empty tissue box with an opening big enough so your cat's head does not get stuck. Free-feed your cat by placing dry food in different locations around the house and letting her use her natural hunting instinct to find it. This will help when your cat gets you up at night because she is hungry. It is also a great way to encourage active behavior. Whichever of these methods you use, be sure that your cat is getting enough to eat.

Toys and Games

Most cats are attracted to things that move. Soft toys, particularly those on the end of strings, are often great fun. It is important to rotate toys so the cat does not become bored with the same toys all the time. Try using a toy box and varying the toys to which the cat has access each day.

There are many games that you can play with your cat, and it is a matter of finding out what interests her. Games that involve chasing and movement are quite popular. You can also play a video on your TV or computer that shows images of birds, fish, and other fun things for the cat to sit and watch. These videos are made especially for cats and can entertain her when no one is home.

Interacting with the Outside World

Providing your cat with access to the outside world is important. One way to do this is by setting up a secure outdoor play enclosure. Several companies make these types of enclosures, which provide safe and fun outdoor areas for cats.

Providing your cat with "window TV" is a great way to keep her entertained while she experiences additional mental and emotional enrichment. Cats love to look out windows and watch birds at bird feeders or birdbaths. Place one of these items by a window where your cat can easily see it. She will watch the birds for hours.

If you train your cat to walk on a secure cat harness and lead, you can then take her outside into the yard for fully supervised play. Never let your cat outside without supervision and a properly fitted harness and leash. It is dangerous outside for a cat. (See Chapter 14.)

← **A seat by the window will keep your cat entertained and his mind stimulated.**

Bring the Outside In

Bring a novel smell, such as grass clippings in a small bag, indoors. If you bring plants into the home, be sure they are not toxic to your cat. Find a list of plants that are toxic to cats on the ASPCA's website: *www.aspca.org/pet-care/animal-poison-control*.

An indoor garden can be fun for a cat to explore, scratch, and nibble. Plants and seeds of catmint, catnip, and cat grass are available from pet shops and garden centers. Be sure that your cat reacts in a positive way when using catnip.

Vertical Space

Cats love climbing and having access to high places, so create climbing and resting areas at different levels around the house. This is especially beneficial if you have more than one cat. Building cat-sized staircases, ramps, and platforms around a room for cats to climb is another great way to enable them to be at different heights. Scratching posts can also satisfy your cat's desire to scratch and climb.

Social Enrichment

Cats are social animals that need to have social interaction every day. You can provide social interaction by petting, handling, or playing with your cat, or just by hanging out with her on the sofa. Interaction with another cat or dog in your home is also a wonderful way to allow your cat to be social, which is why having more than one pet is often beneficial to cats.

Shelters, such as the ARL, have developed programs to promote double cat adoptions. We believe it is in the best emotional and physical interest of a cat for her to have a friend. Two or more cats keep each other company and will play

→ **A multiple-level scratching post can satisfy several of a cat's needs.**

and interact. Shelters also often try to adopt bonded pairs to the same home, meaning that if cats came into the shelter together, they will be adopted together.

Training Enrichment

A huge myth is that cats cannot be trained. The truth is that you can teach your cat to sit, to come, to walk in a harness, and much more. This provides your cat with mental stimulation and makes life more interesting for her. All training should be positive, with rewards given for appropriate behaviors.

Natural Enrichment

Natural enrichment can be defined as anything your cat or kitten likes to do to entertain herself without your being involved. Provide your cat with areas and items to express natural behaviors, including rubbing, scratching, climbing, chasing, hunting, running, and playing. For example, hang a toy for your cat to stalk, chase, and attack. Natural behaviors are as varied as cats' personalities, so watch your cat, learn what she likes, and help her release her inner lioness.

MEWSINGS

Catnip

Q: I take my cat, Bunny, outside on a harness/tether in the spring and summer. I work in my part of the garden while Bunny plays in her area, which has a large patch of catnip. When we come back inside, Bunny becomes angry and attacks me. I don't know why she acts like this.

A: Some cats experience personality changes around catnip. Bunny was becoming overstimulated by the catnip. When they went inside, Bunny was so geared up that she would become aggressive with her owner. Limit the amount of catnip your cat gets at a time. One way to do this is to buy a catnip toy. Let your cat play with it for a set period of time before you pick it up and put it in a drawer until later. Another idea is to get a catnip plant and break off a small quantity of the catnip to give to your cat.

HAPPY ENDINGS

Tank and Bear

When we were back home in Iowa for the holidays, Michelle suggested we go to the ARL and take a look at the cats. I knew the second we walked in that we would be leaving with a cat. I was surprised to learn that cats thrive in pairs. As we walked through the cat area, we saw four little kittens sleeping in their beds. As Michelle and I watched, we noticed that the black kitten (Tank) was the most ornery and least likely to settle down. The striped kitten (Bear) looked as if he were rolling his eyes at Tank. Michelle wanted to meet them both. After ten seconds in the room with them, I was sold, and Michelle was out the door to sign the adoption papers.

Tank loves water and is often spotted on the tub ledge, just out of reach of the shower spray. He has also developed a love of washing his paws in his separate paw-washing water bowl. He is the resident escape artist who loves to run out the door and into the hallway of our apartment building. Tank has developed major-league skills at playing fetch, and he cannot resist the urge to tear up toilet paper or paper towels whenever we leave them out.

Bear is such a sweetheart. He is independent and a champ at cuddling. He never passes up a chance to sit on our laps as we work on the computer or watch TV. He loves to have his nose rubbed and is always the first to warm up to visitors, usually by jumping on their laps. He is also probably the cleanest cat around and the first to run to the sound of the treat bag opening.

Tank and Bear are an investigative duo who love to sniff groceries, pounce on boxes, and wrestle. They also enjoy a good game of chicken with the vacuum cleaner. There is no doubt these two are brothers, as they can be found wrestling one moment and cuddling the next. We have loved watching our kittens grow up and spending time with them.

—the Bonnemas

8 Cats and Wild Play

Rough, play-motivated behaviors are common in active cats younger than two years of age as well as in cats that live in one-cat households. Playing allows your cat the opportunity to practice her survival skills. Rough play occurs when your cat moves from a play-motivated emotional state to a predatory state, using her claws, teeth, or both when overstimulated. Even though she may be practicing her survival skills, she needs to learn what behavior is appropriate with humans.

Kittens are curious and like to explore new areas. They also like to investigate all moving objects, people, and other pets. They may bat, bite, and pounce on objects to learn about them. A kitten learns how to soften her bite from her mother and littermates. A kitten that is separated from her family too early may play more wildly than a kitten that has had the benefit of learning the rules from her cat family.

You can create behavior problems in a kitten by using your hands or feet, instead of appropriate toys, when playing, because you are teaching the kitten that rough play with people is acceptable.

DID YOU KNOW?

Kittens learn from each other, so if there is room in your family you should consider getting another kitten. They will teach each other how to play appropriately. We recommend at least a double-cat household.

Encouraging Appropriate Behavior

In most cases, you can teach your kitten or young adult cat that rough play is not desirable behavior. If your kitten or cat begins to chew on your fingers or toes, redirect her aggressive behavior onto acceptable objects, such as cat toys. Drag a toy along the floor to encourage your kitten to pounce on it instead of on you. Try throwing a ball away from your kitten so that she can chase it—she might even bring it back to be thrown again. A ping-pong ball works great because it is lightweight and will bounce and roll for a long time, keeping your kitten entertained. (If you also have a dog, be careful, because dogs tend to crush ping-pong balls.)

A stuffed toy about the same size as your kitten can make a great playmate. She can wrestle with it, grab it with both front feet, bite it, and kick it with her back feet, just like she did with her littermates when they were young. She will try to play with human feet and hands in the same way, so it is important to provide an alternative

↑ Kittens are full of curiosity and energy.

↑ To a cat, your fingers and hands can be enticing playthings unless you teach her otherwise.

play target. Encourage your kitten to play with a stuffed toy by rubbing it against her belly when she starts to play roughly. As soon as she accepts the toy, move your hand out of the way.

Kittens need a lot of playtime. Set up three or four consistent times during the day to initiate play. Playing with your kitten often and teaching her the playtime rules will help her understand that she doesn't have to be the one to initiate play by pouncing on you.

Discouraging Inappropriate Behavior

Set rules for your kitten's behavior from day one. If you do not have rules, your kitten will make her own. Every person your cat comes in contact with, including visitors, should know and reinforce these rules. Remember, your kitten cannot be expected to understand that it is acceptable to play rough with Dad but not with the baby, so no one in the family should allow it. Set rules that the whole family can follow to help your kitten adjust her play style. She will eventually understand how far she can go if you are consistent. Keep in mind that none of the following methods will be effective unless you give your kitten acceptable outlets for her energy.

Be Consistent

Always be consistent in redirecting your kitten's rough play. Do not allow her to bite your hand one day and then scold her for it the next day. This only confuses the kitten and makes it more difficult to teach her appropriate behavior.

DO NOT...

Do not tap, flick, or hit your kitten for rough play. These actions are almost always guaranteed to backfire. Your kitten could become afraid of you or interpret those flicks as play, which could result in even more rough behavior. Squirt bottles are also a bad idea, since using them can make your kitten afraid of you.

Picking your out-of-control kitten up for a "time out" could reinforce the undesirable behavior, because she probably likes when you pick her up and will view it as a reward.

Seek Help

If your kitten is biting or scratching through your skin, seek immediate help from a behavior specialist. Keep your kitten confined to a room so she cannot continue the unwanted behavior until you can get help. Thoroughly clean all bites and scratches and consult your physician, as cat-inflicted wounds can easily become infected.

↑ **If your kitten is busy with her toys, she won't be causing mischief.**

- Supply her with appropriate toys, plenty of playtime, or a kitten playmate to encourage good behavior from the start.
- If your kitten starts to play roughly, stop the play.
- If distraction and redirection techniques don't seem to be working, withdraw all attention from the kitten by walking away and leaving her alone in the room.
- When withdrawing attention, do not pick the kitten up and move her to another room; she will view that as a reward because she probably likes when you pick her up.

Play Biting

Q: My three-and-a-half-year-old cat, Buddy, bites my feet and then runs away. I have tried to stop his behavior by spraying him with a water bottle and by pushing him away, but it doesn't work. How can I teach him to stop this behavior?

A: Buddy is obviously "play biting." Spraying him and pushing him away will only escalate his behavior. When a cat is playing and someone uses a hand or foot to push the cat away, the cat reads it as the human engaging in play with him. The hand motion and interaction tells the cat that the "game is on." Typically, cats will actually escalate their play behavior to match what they perceive to the human's level of play.

Water bottles, while commonly used in the past to train cats not to do something, actually have a negative effect. The cat sees his guardian spraying him with water and becomes fearful.

We want cats to build up their relationships with their humans, so we want to use positive, not negative, tactics to redirect our cats' behavior. After explaining this to Buddy's owner, we discussed a new plan that involved using ping-pong balls to encourage desired behavior. After a short period of time, Buddy chased after the ball that his owner tossed until the ball became more fun that biting at feet.

Nipping Solutions

Q: My cat Marlene is nine months old. She has started to nip at my hands while she sits on my lap. What can I do to get her to stop biting me?

A: In essence, Marlene is playing, even though it seems like aggression. There are three main ways to change this behavior. The first is to "hiss" at Marlene when she bites. It is important to do this at the exact moment she is biting you. Marlene's mother would have used hissing to correct Marlene's inappropriate behavior when she was a young kitten, so it often works for humans to do the same thing; rarely will the cat look at you and go back to what she was doing after you hiss at her. She will likely jump off your lap or move away from you quickly, and this is the reaction you want. It tells you that the cat has received the message that her behavior was inappropriate.

The second suggestion is to redirect her play from you to toys. Ping-pong balls are a good choice because they are lightweight and they bounce. The moment you see Marlene getting ready to bite in play, toss the ball across her line of sight, and she will run after the ball instead of biting you.

The third and best suggestion is to get a feline friend for Marlene. The sex of the cats is not an issue, but try to get a cat between six months and two years of age so the two cats have similar energy and play drive. As an only cat, Marlene is lonely and wants to play—and play hard! The two cats will teach each other what is appropriate and what is too wild.

9 Scratching

Scratching is a perfectly normal and necessary feline behavior. Although scratching does serve to shorten and condition cats' claws, cats scratch for the primary reasons of marking their territory and stretching. Cats may also threaten or play by swiping their paws. For cats that live primarily outdoors, scratching is seldom a problem for their owners because scratching is usually directed at appropriate objects such as tree trunks or fence posts. Play-swatting with other cats seldom leads to injuries, because cats have fairly thick skin and coats for protection. When play does get a little rough, cats are good at sorting things out between themselves. On occasion, rough play or territorial fighting leads to injuries or abscesses that require veterinary attention.

Cats that live primarily or exclusively indoors may run into trouble with their owners when they begin to scratch furniture, walls, and doors, or when they use their claws to climb or hang from the drapes. Claws can also cause injuries to people when the cats are overly playful or don't like a particular type of handling or restraint. With a good understanding of cat behavior and a bit of effort, it is possible to prevent or avoid most scratching problems.

It is impractical and unfair to expect cats to stop scratching entirely. Cats that spend most of their time indoors will require an area for indoor scratching, climbing, and playing. While it may not be possible to stop a cat from scratching, it is possible to redirect behavior to appropriate indoor areas. Building or designing

↑ **Start a nail-trimming routine with your kitten so she gets used to the procedure.**

a scratching post, providing a cat tree and other appropriate toys, and keeping the cat away from potential problem areas are usually adequate measures when dealing with most scratching problems.

Trimming Claws

You may be able to lessen some of your cat's potential for destruction by carefully trimming her claws. It is important to have your veterinarian show you how to trim them. Trimming claws is a relatively simple task, if you know how to do it correctly. If you do it incorrectly and cut the "quick" (the vein that runs through each nail), it will be painful for your cat. While the area will physically heal, such an injury could make your cat fearful of claw trims.

Take your time and start by trimming one paw at a time and building from there. Teach your cat

Other Activities

Provide your cat with other stimulation to keep him occupied throughout the day. For ideas, see Chapter 7.

When choosing or making a scratching post, look at the surfaces of the scratched furniture. The surface of the post should be covered with a similar material.

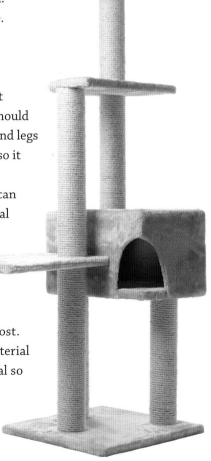

that having his claws trimmed is fun and rewarding by offering him a favorite treat as you trim. Ideally, you should trim your cat's claws every few weeks.

If you have a kitten, start trimming early. Teaching your kitten to sit still during claw trimming will be easier if he grows up thinking that this is a normal routine. You can also teach an older cat to sit relatively still while having his claws trimmed. Patience and going slowly will help him accept the procedure.

How to Design a Scratching Area

Because cats also use their scratching posts for marking and stretching, posts should be set up in prominent areas with at least one post close to the cat's sleeping quarters. The post should be tall enough for the cat to scratch while standing on her hind legs with her forelegs extended. It should also be sturdy enough so it does not topple when scratched.

Some cats prefer a scratching post with a corner so they can scratch two sides at once. Other cats may prefer a horizontal scratching post. Some scratching posts are even designed to be wall-mounted or hung on a door. It is important to observe your cat's scratching behavior and preferences to determine what type of scratching post will be best for her.

Give special consideration to the surface texture of the post. Commercial posts are often covered with tightly woven material for durability, but many cats prefer a loosely woven material so

→ **Scratching posts with perches and a variety of textures create an interesting play area for your cat.**

that their claws can hook onto and tear the material during scratching. Scratching is also a marking behavior, and cats want to leave visual marks. Carpet may be an acceptable covering, but comb it first to make sure that there are no tight loops.

Some cats prefer sisal, burlap, a piece of fabric from an old chair, or even bare wood for scratching. Be certain to use a material that appeals to your cat.

↑ **A scratching post can prevent damage to your furniture, carpets, curtains, and more.**

Getting Your Cat to Use a Post

A good way to get your cat to use the scratching post is to turn the scratching area into an interesting and desirable play center. Perches to climb on, spaces to climb into, and toys mounted on ropes or springs are all highly appealing to most cats. Placing a few toys, cardboard boxes, catnip treats, or even the food bowl in the area should help keep the cat interested. Sometimes rubbing the post with tuna oil or catnip will increase its appeal. You can also give the cat food rewards when you observe her scratching at her post. Products

Cat Scratch Fever

There is a disease called "cat scratch fever," caused by *Bartonella* bacteria, that can be passed from cats to humans. This disease is believed to be transmitted by cat scratches, cat bites, or exposure to the saliva of an infected cat. Symptoms may appear about two to three weeks after the infection. Common human symptoms include a blister at the site of the injury (this is usually the first sign), fatigue, fever, headache, swollen lymph node near the scratch or bite, and overall discomfort.

Generally, cat scratch fever is not serious, and medical treatment is not always needed. In severe cases, or in people with compromised immune systems, treatment with antibiotics usually leads to recovery.

Cheek Marking

Cats and kittens also mark by rubbing their cheeks on people or objects, such as furniture and trees, secreting scent from glands on their faces and heads. Unlike scratching, cheek marking does not leave a visual mark. This scent marking can define territory or ownership of areas and objects, including you.

have been designed to reward a cat automatically by dispensing food rewards each time the cat scratches.

It may be necessary to place the post in the center of a room or near the furniture that the cat was previously trying to scratch until she reliably uses the post. You can then move it to a less obtrusive location. For some cats, multiple posts in several locations may be necessary.

Inappropriate Scratching

Indirect, nonphysical forms of correcting your cat's behavior may be useful, particularly if you can remain out of sight while administering it. In this way, the cat may learn that scratching is unpleasant even when you are not present. Avoid all forms of physical punishment because it can cause your cat to become fearful or aggressive toward you. At best, the cat will learn to stop inappropriate scratching only when you are around. The best deterrents are those that train the pet not to scratch inappropriate objects at all, even in your absence.

If you can make the target of your cat's inappropriate scratching less appealing, the cat will likely seek out a

↑ **Plastic carpet runner with the bumpy side out is an effective deterrent to scratching.**

Do Not Declaw

Declawing is not an acceptable option to stop your cat from scratching. It is literally a form of maiming a cat. In many countries, declawing is illegal and considered inhumane. Declawing can lead to physical, emotional, and behavioral complications. Some cats can develop an aversion to their litter boxes because of the pain associated with scratching in the litter after a declawing procedure. Declawing is not a trivial procedure, like trimming the claws is. A cat's claws are a vital part of her anatomy, essential to balance, mobility, and survival, that should not be removed.

new area for scratching, which we hope will be her scratching post. An environmental negative is something in the environment that will cause your cat to have a negative association with a particular area, for example, double-sided tape. The benefit of an environmental negative is that it will not affect the relationship you have with your cat, because, to the cat, you were not involved.

The simplest approach is to cover the surface you don't want your cat to scratch with a less appealing material. Carpet runner plastic turned wrong side up, a loosely draped piece of fabric, aluminum foil, or double-sided tape will work.

Another effective deterrent is to "booby-trap" problem areas so scratching or even just approaching the area is unpleasant for the cat.

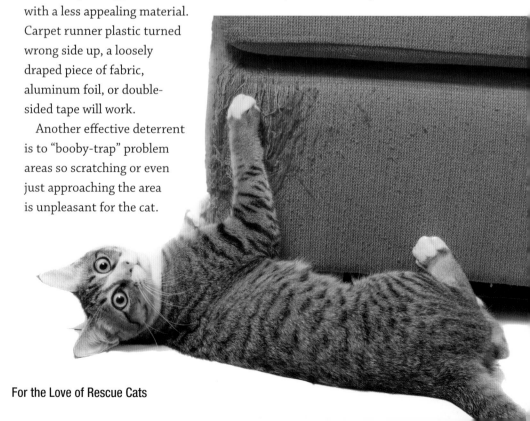

↑ **With vinyl caps applied, the cat's front claws cannot inflict damage.**

Motion detectors or a stack of plastic cups set to topple when the cat scratches will work; you just need to be certain that any traps you set up will not hurt your cat.

Another way to prevent inappropriate scratching is to glue vinyl caps to your cat's front claws. These are available in a kit and are easy to use. The vinyl caps are generally applied to the front paws only because these claws are what cause most of the destruction to your home. One application of the caps lasts approximately three to six months, depending on your cat. After applying them, check your cat's claws weekly.

Points to Remember

- Don't declaw!
- Understand your cat's need to scratch.
- Do not punish your cat for inappropriate scratching; it does not work.
- Provide a suitable place for your cat to scratch, and make the scratching post attractive to the cat in height and texture.
- Make the place where your cat has been inappropriately scratching unattractive by using physical or scent-related deterrents.
- Ask your veterinarian to show you how to trim your cat's claws properly.
- Whenever possible, start trimming your cat's claws when she is young.

Try a New Post

Q: My cat Sam scratches my furniture. I am considering declawing him or turning him into an outside cat. The scratching post I have sits on the floor, is covered with carpet and is horizontal in design.

A: Sam was scratching the couch in a vertical motion on one of the arms, so I advised his owner to get an upright scratching post covered in sisal and place it close to the spot on the couch where Sam was scratching. I also suggested that she sprinkle catnip on the post to attract Sam to it. I told her that if Sam started using the couch, then she should go over and move him nicely to the nearby post.

After trying this approach for one day, the owner called me and told me that she had done what I suggested. The first time Sam scratched the couch, she had moved him to the new post, and he immediately had started using the post. I told her to make sure that the new approach continued to work.

After a few days, she called to report that Sam was using the new post and things were working out well. In this case, Sam's owner was good about monitoring Sam after the new scratching post came home and redirecting him to the desired place to scratch. She also rewarded Sam with verbal praise and food treats a few times to reinforce that he was scratching in the appropriate place.

HAPPY ENDINGS

Max and Mr. Knightly

My house was in need of a cat a few months after my seventeen-year-old kitty passed away. On a busy Saturday morning I visited the main office of the ARL to look at the kitties. I wanted a cat that was different from my previous cat, a gray striped tabby. In the back room, I found him: a sixteen-week-old red-gold male going by the name of Tabby. I knew he was the one when I held him and got no complaints.

I went back to the shelter later that day to finalize the paperwork and bring the carrier. Tabby (renamed Maximan or "Max") settled in immediately when I brought him home, and he even delighted my guests at a party a few days later. He took to a harness without any trouble and amazes many people by walking on his leash.

Max is an extremely smart cat that can get into anything. He can open any door that isn't latched by either pushing or pulling it. Because Max is so smart, his little brain is going all the time, and he can become bored, demanding attention and often playing rough. He needed something to keep him occupied during the day.

Four years after adopting Max, I stopped by a local pet-supply store that happened to be holding cat adoptions that day. In the middle cage was a big, white cat named Wizard. He was declawed, had medium-length hair, and was five years old. I could not believe someone hadn't already snatched him up. I wanted that cat, but I already had Max and didn't really think I needed two cats, although Max might like some company.

It took a couple of days for me to decide that I really could handle a second cat. Another day passed before I could adopt Wizard, but he was obviously meant to be mine. I called him Mr. Knightly, hoping he would be a good influence on Maximan.

I discovered that Mr. Knightly had some health issues. His digestive system was out of whack and he was stressed. His body was bloated and hard, and he threw up daily in addition to having runny and bloody stools. A couple of trips to the vet didn't dramatically improve things; however, he did slowly begin to improve with a consistent diet and stable surroundings.

It took at least six months for Mr. Knightly to settle into his new home—much longer than I would have guessed—but Maximan and Mr. Knightly became buddies. They run, jump, and play together and have a system worked out for who gets to sit in the window and who gets the prime spot on the bed. Two successful adoptions!

—Amy

10 Communicating with Your Cat

Who Says Your Cat Can't Talk to You?

Cats do communicate with their owners. Some cats never make a sound, while others meow, chirp, and otherwise vocalize on a regular basis. What type of communication and the frequency depend on the cat. There are even specific cat breeds that tend to vocalize more than others. When you work around multiple cats at an animal shelter or live with more than one cat, the differences in the cats' vocalization patterns are clearly noticeable.

Cats make sounds for different reasons, from trying to get their owners' attention at dinnertime to conveying that they are not feeling well physically or emotionally. The underlying reasons as to why cats vocalize vary from cat to cat, but in every case it is an attempt at communicating with their humans or other animals in their household.

In the following explanations of the different types of cat communication, I can use my own cat in many of the examples. I live with seven cats, and they all communicate in different ways and for different reasons.

Nontalkative: Oscar is a medium-coated domestic cat that has not made a sound as long as I have had him. He purrs when I pet him or when he lies beside me, but otherwise, as the saying goes, he is as quiet as a church mouse.

Breed: Gracie is a Siamese cat that was abandoned on my porch when she was six weeks old. She meows "hello" every time she sees me and when she wants attention. When I began researching, I found out quickly that the Siamese breed is known for being talkative. When people ask me what breed of cat to adopt, I tell them to realize

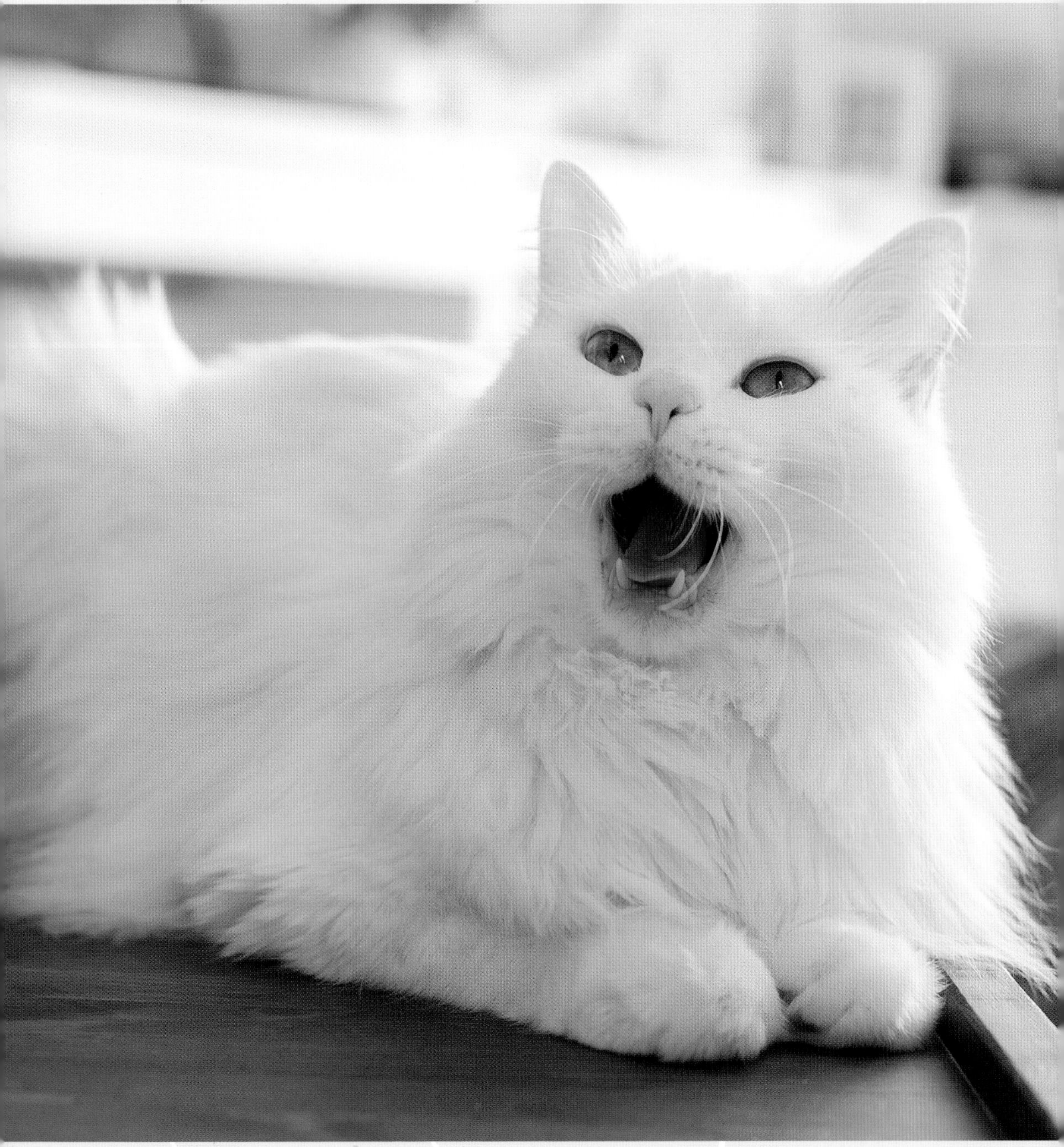

↑   **Siamese cats are among the chattier breeds.**

that some cats are known to be more vocal than others and that they should consider this characteristic when choosing a cat. Different cat breeds have different traits.

Mealtime: Stitch is a domestic shorthair who meows as if the world is ending if his food bowl is nearly empty. He came to me as a stray and was starving, so food is important to Stitch. He meows "hello" every now and again, but an almost-empty food bowl gets Stitch meowing and howling until I fill the bowl.

Medical: Beso is a Havana Brown that is relatively quiet, except when he is sick. When he is not feeling well, he meows often, very quietly, to make sure that I know he is under the weather.

Jack is a domestic shorthair. Since he turned seventeen, he has started yowling sporadically. After a few visits to the vet to make sure that he wasn't sick, we determined that old age was causing Jack to make these horrible noises. When he begins to yowl, I just pet him until he quiets down.

Warning: Bella is a calico cat that never meows. However, she does growl quite loudly when she sees Gracie, her cat housemate. They are not fans of each other, and Bella will instantly start growling when she sees Gracie. She is

Cat Fact

A cat can make more than 100 different sounds.

communicating a warning to Gracie to get away. Unfortunately, Gracie rarely listens.

Talkative: Ocho is a domestic shorthair cat that is completely deaf. He talks more than any other cat I have, and he uses different vocals and ranges depending on his message. For example, when he sees that I am home, he meows a simple "hello." If he gets locked out of the bedroom at night, he will meow loudly for as long as it takes for me to open the door for him to come in. When I do open the door (and I know I shouldn't if I want him to stop meowing!), he comes in and changes to a scolding tone for leaving him out. Then he will come and lie down by me and start to softly meow and purr to let me know that all is forgiven.

Grief: It has been reiterated to me over the years that a cat's meow can be caused by grief. The loss of another pet in the home or settling into a new home and feeling insecure can be a source of grief. The best thing to do is keep your cat to her regular schedule and pet and talk to her in a calm and soothing voice. The meowing will decrease and eventually cease.

Attention seeking: We receive a handful of calls or emails every year from pet owners whose cats' meowing drives them crazy! Depending on the reason for the meowing, one of the most consistent things you can do is not react. If your cat meows to get you to pet her, and you pet her, she is going to keep meowing because it has worked in the past to get your attention. Instead, get up and walk away or completely ignore her. When your cat is quiet, then pet her. This reinforces that meowing gets her nothing, but being quiet gets her what she wants.

Whatever the reason for your cat's vocalizations, it is important as a loving owner that you try to understand. Then, when something is wrong, you will hear what your cat is trying to tell you.

← "Hey! I'm over here!"

DID YOU KNOW?

In most cases, scolding a cat to keep her quiet will do nothing. The very fact that you are talking to her will keep them talking to you, no matter what tone of voice you are using.

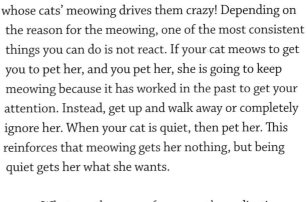

↑ Relaxed and content, this cat enjoys some cuddles.

Cat Body Language

We wish our cats could tell us how they feel and what they need—and actually they do. We just have to learn to "talk cat."

A cat's main method of communication is through body language. Cats also use some vocal communication because they know it will get our attention. The great thing about cats is they act how they feel and feel how they act. They have no reason to lie, so if they want a pat, they will let you know. The same goes for when they are upset or frightened. We need to listen to our cats. The more you observe your cat, the better you will be at reading her body language.

Cat Fact

Watch your cat's hair. It will stand up evenly all over her body when she is scared. When she feels defensive or threatened, and getting ready to attack, the hair stands up along the spine and tail.

Body Language Signals

Relaxed cat: When your cat is relaxed, her body will be soft and free of muscle tension with her whiskers in a neutral position. The tail will be in a neutral position, and the eyes may be squinting and blinking regularly. In many cases, she may be purring. However, it is good to remember that some cats purr when they are stressed.

Fearful cat: When frightened, a cat will likely try to hide and escape. If she feels threatened and can't escape to a safe place up high or under something, she may show some or all of the following:

- Muscles tensed, ready for flight or fight
- Eyes fixed on the threat and pupils dilated
- Body crouched down
- Ears flattened
- Tail low
- Chin drawn in

If the cat rolls on her side or back while showing these signs, stay away. This is your last warning before the teeth and claws come out.

DID YOU KNOW?

Cats show contentment by using a kneading motion, which is often accompanied by purring.

↑   The cat under your bed may be hiding from something that scares her.

Defensive cat: A defensive cat believes she has little choice but to defend herself. You may just be trying to be friendly, but the cat's perception is different. The cat may exhibit the same characteristics as a fearful cat.

Stimulated cat: This may occur when you are playing with or petting your cat. She may become stimulated, which is generally a good thing, and it means the cat is having fun. However, make sure that she does not become overstimulated. Look for these signs:

- Face tightened
- Vocalizations
- Fur fluffed up
- Tail flicking back and forth

Decoding Your Cat's Emotions

There is a lot to observe when interpreting your cat's emotions. Just like anything else we learn, it takes time. Most of us know when our friends or family members get upset. After some observation and time, you should also be able to decode your cat's signals. Causes of emotional distress include:

- Changes in physical environment
- Anything that acutely startles the cat, such as loud noises
- Unpredictable and unfamiliar manipulations or handling
- Lack of choices or control over situations
- Irregular and unpredictable feeding times (for example, being hungry for extended periods)

→ **Ears flattened and pupils dilated are two physical signs of fear.**

When looking at your cat's body language, don't rely on only one communication signal. Look at the whole cat, as well as the environment around you. Is there anything that may be causing a change in your cat's behavior? It is important to look at all behaviors in context.

Ever wonder why your cat jumps on the lap of the guest who doesn't like cats? It is because someone who doesn't like cats will do things that cats like during greetings: he or she will squint, turn his or her head away, and avoid direct contact with the cat. To the cat, this person is saying hello and being nonthreatening. Sure enough, the cat ends up in this person's lap!

- Irregular and unpredictable cleaning of litter boxes
- Absence of stroking, petting or other positive interactions with humans
- Changes in social environment (such as new baby, new roommate, change in owner's work schedule)
- Lack of mental stimulation
  Indicators of emotional distress include:
- Increased hiding or attempts to hide
- Decreased social interaction
- Decreased grooming
- Decreased active exploration and play behavior
- Greater proportion of daily time spent awake (exhibiting vigilance and scanning behavior)

HAPPY ENDINGS

Charlie

When we adopted a younger cat, we noticed that our older cats were not interested in playing with her. After talking to the ARL cat behaviorist, we decided to adopt another cat, one closer to her age, to be her buddy. I went to the ARL website to look at adoptable younger cats, and I chose four for my husband and I to meet. We fell in love with all four cats but decided to adopt Charlie because he had been waiting the longest for a home.

He is a big brown tabby with tons of personality. He acclimated to our home with ease. Charlie enjoys belly rubs and sitting on the screened porch, and he loves food. We have to hide the cat treats in the freezer because he learned how to open the cupboards and was serving himself treats at all hours of the day and night. Just thinking about Charlie makes me smile. He is curious and smart, and he loves to play. He is a great addition to our family, and I love him.

—Lora

Felix

Felix belonged to an elderly lady who passed away. None of her grandkids could take him, so they gave him to the ARL. While working at ARL South, I felt so bad for him. He was extremely skinny and frightened, and he cried all the time. Felix also had the most unusual silver fur with reddish tabby markings. He was too unique and sad not to take home. He is my baby now, and I've "fattened" him up to a normal weight. He greets me at the door and always tries to "help" with whatever I am doing, whether it is laundry or cooking. While my other cat doesn't appreciate him, Felix and my dog love to wrestle and chase each other. Felix also loves to try to share my food, usually sticking his head right into my plate or cereal bowl. He went from

the shelter to being a king and living in the lap of luxury. He is an integral part of my life now, and I don't know what I would do without him.

—Blaine and Alyssa

HAPPY ENDINGS

Mitch

A coworker was considering adopting a cat and asked me to go to the ARL with her. I already had two cats, so I thought I was safe in accompanying her. We met a sweet one-and-a-half-year-old male with a little stump of a tail. We were told he had come in as a stray. We spent time cuddling and playing with him.

The next day, my coworker decided that it wasn't a good time for her to adopt a cat. I was in trouble. All I could think about was that sweet cat with the little tail stump that would wiggle around. After spending only a short time with this cat, I was attached to him. That day, I became an official rescue mom and Mitch (my new cat) got two new brothers.

For the first couple of days, Mitch spent his time in my study. I would let him out when I was home so he could get used to his new brothers. There was some establishment of the pecking order, but they all adapted fairly quickly. Mitch and I, on the other hand, had a bit more of a challenge. I could tell he had been abused. He wouldn't let me walk up to him, and if I tried to reach down and pet him, he would cringe. I talked to him a lot so he would get used to my voice. I also found that if I sat on the floor and held my hand out, he would come up to me.

After a few months, Mitch started sleeping with me and even coming up and sitting on my lap. He would meet me at the door when I came home and then flop on the floor and want me to pet his belly. After having him for a year and a half, I can't imagine our family without him. Even on my worst day, he always has the power to cheer me up. I'm thrilled to have provided a forever home for a deserving kitty, and I would recommend anyone else to do the same.

—Crystal

11 The Fearful Cat

There are a range of reasons that cats develop fears, and many of these fears are manageable. Following are some of the reasons.

Socialization: A cat may have had limited exposure to other animals and people when young. Socialization is an important aspect of raising a kitten. The socialization window for kittens starts to close at twelve weeks of age. Without adequate, continual, and positive interaction with people and other animals, cats may develop fears.

Negative experiences: A cat can learn fear from just one negative event. You may not have thought that a particular experience was a big deal, but it might have been traumatic from the cat's perspective. This experience may stick with the cat in similar future situations. For example, a negative event with a small child could result in a cat that is fearful of all small children.

Likewise, unpleasant events associated with a person or animal can sometimes lead to increasing fear. For example, if a cat is punished or if something frightening happens in the presence of a particular person or other animal, the cat may begin to associate that person or animal with the punishment or negative occurrence.

Genetics: Genetics are another important contributing factor to the development of fear. Some cats are inherently timid and fearful, and these animals may never become outgoing and social.

↑ The earliest socialization starts with the mother cat and littermates.

Identifying Your Cat's Fears

When your cat is frightened, he may try to appear smaller, place his ears back, stay immobile, and want to hide. In addition, he may show signs of agitation or aggression, such as dilated pupils, arched back, piloerection (hair standing on end), hissing, or growling.

DID YOU KNOW?

Balloons, plastic bags, and loud noises are common fears among cats.

Before you seek any behavioral help, visit your veterinarian and get a complete medical examination, including bloodwork, for your cat to determine if there is a medical condition contributing to the behavior problem. If there are no medical problems, and your cat shows extreme fear or aggression, you'll need a behavioral consultation with your veterinarian, a veterinary behaviorist, or an animal behavior specialist.

For a cat with mild fear, your intervention may help prevent her fear from worsening. Begin by identifying

↑ **Dilated pupils and an arched back indicate a fearful cat.**

the cause of your cat's fear. Sometimes, a cat will have multiple fears. In either case, identifying the cause is not always easy and needs to be exact. You will need to determine exactly what makes the cat afraid, as well as where the fearful behavior occurs. Often, there are certain situations, people, animals, objects, or places that provoke the fearful behavior more than others. For treatment to be successful, it is important to identify and work around the least likely as well as the most likely causes of the fear.

DID YOU KNOW?

Shelter cats have no more predisposition to fear than stray cats or cats acquired through breeders or friends. Adopting a cat is always the way to go!

↑ Food rewards can help a cat turn a negative into a positive.

A Plan of Action

Before you can begin a behavior modification program, you must be able to control your cat. You can accomplish this with a figure-eight harness and leash or, if needed, a wire crate.

Next, pair the fearful situation with food rewards to create a positive association for the cat. The goal of this training is to encourage the cat to assume a relaxed and happy body posture and facial expression in the presence of the fear trigger. If the association with the fear factor can be turned into a positive one, your cat should gradually develop a positive attitude when exposed to it over time.

A program of counterconditioning and desensitization is also useful for training your cat to handle situations she finds fearful. *Desensitization* is a process of gradual exposure to a fearful stimulus. That sounds fancy, but, putting it simply, it involves getting the cat accustomed to the fearful stimulus little by little, in a slow and compassionate manner, until she sees that there is nothing to fear and can settle down.

Desensitization involves controlled exposure to situations or stimuli that might cause fear at minimal enough levels that your cat can still take treats or play games during the exposure. Therefore, this helps the cat associate the fearful stimulus with having fun. The aim of desensitization, in combination with counterconditioning, is to change a pet's attitude or feelings about a stimulus from one that is negative to one that is positive. If, at any stage, your cat stops taking the treats or stops playing, it means that you have gone too far too soon with the stimulus. In this case, allow the cat to leave the area if she desires.

Counterconditioning is used to change the cat's response to a person, animal, or situation in a gradual but progressive way. This is done by training the cat to perform or display an acceptable response, such as play or food acquisition, each time she is exposed to the thing she fears. Rather than attempting to overcome her fear all at once, you set up the training to expose the cat to the objects of her fear at levels of reduced intensity to ensure a successful outcome. You encourage and reward desirable responses so the cat develops a new, more desirable, behavior in response to the fearful stimulus. If you can successfully divert the cat's attention, you can then reward the appropriate response. Again, never push training to the point where the cat feels the need to escape.

↑   **Make sure that your kitten's experiences are positive and nonthreatening.**

Your Reactions

Owner responses, such as anxiety, fear, a raised voice, or any form of punishment will only increase your pet's fear or anxiety. Similarly, a fear- or anxiety-inducing stimulus presented to your cat will further aggravate her anxiety. Be sure to retrain with calm control.

The goal of training is to reinforce appropriate, desirable responses. Therefore, it is critical that you do not give rewards while the cat is displaying an inappropriate response. Of course, if there is any chance of injury, quickly and safely removing your cat from the situation becomes your priority.

If you have a kitten, the most important thing is to prevent fear through early, frequent, and pleasant interactions with people of all ages. Due to the role of genetics in developing future fears, try to select a nonfearful, sociable kitten. Take your time and look at your prospective kitten's behavior traits. Likewise, if you are able to assess and observe the kitten's parents, you may gain insight into the type of personality that the kitten may develop as she grows up.

MEWSINGS

The Disappearing Cat

Q: What can I do about my cat, Tess? She is afraid of kids, and whenever my grandkids come over, she disappears somewhere in the house and I cannot find her.

A: A cat that is afraid and removes herself from a situation should be left alone. It's a big mistake to pull a cat out of her hiding place and bring her to the fearful stimulus (in this case, the children) to show her that there is nothing to fear. The cat is already afraid and should be allowed to keep herself away from the situation.

If the cat doesn't completely disappear, you can help ease her fear. When the kids appear to stress out the cat, be sure to give them treats to hold in their hands. Have the kids put the treats down in front of the cat (or as close as they can get without her running off). Have the kids walk away. This shows the cat that when the kids come to the house, good things happen—in this case, the good things are the treats.

You can also use a toy, such as a cat's fishing-pole toy, if the cat loves to play. Have the kids wave the fishing pole slowly beside the cat. Hopefully, the cat will start to play, and this also reinforces that when the kids come to the house, good things (playtime!) happen. Never force the cat to interact with the kids if it causes stress. Let the cat hide if she wants and come out when she is ready.

12 Natural Aversives for Cats

When using environmental aversives or things that are natural aversives for cats, remember that one of the challenges to modifying behaviors in cats is that you may have to do a little trial and error. What works as a natural aversive with one cat may not work with all cats. Just as with humans, individual preferences will vary with each cat. The most important thing to remember is that *in no way should aversives be harmful or create fear in your cat.*

Aversives are often the best method to discourage a cat from a particular behavior, but they seldom work without offering a rewarding alternative. For example, if you place double-sided carpet tape on your counter, it will give your cat an unpleasant sensation when she jumps up on it. Her reward for staying off the counter is not experiencing that unpleasantness.

Defining the Term

Aversive: An unpleasant stimulus that causes avoidance of a thing, situation, or behavior. You can use aversives to repel your cat from something or deter certain behavior without harming her.

↑ **If you don't want claw marks on the furniture, you'll need to find alternatives for your cat.**

Textures and Odors

Use unpleasant textures and smells to keep your cat off counters and furniture indoors. You may also use them on any outdoor areas or objects. Remember, aversives are meant to deter, not harm.

Textures
Indoor

Countertops: Place shelf paper, sticky side up, on the countertop when it is not in use. It will only take one or two sticky landings for your cat to decide that the counter is no longer fun. You can also use double-sided carpet tape in the same way.

Furniture: Wrapping chair or table legs with heavy aluminum foil or plastic will deter your cat from scratching the furniture. Scratching is a natural behavior, so be sure to give her a scratching alternative, such as a scratching post. (See Chapter 9.)

Outdoor

Flower beds: Irregularly shaped or sharp rocks and pine cones, firmly set into the dirt, are uncomfortable for your cat's paws. Make sure that the rocks will not cut your cat's skin. This also works with indoor houseplants.

Garden: Chicken wire, set firmly into dirt with the sharp edges rolled under, will keep your cat from digging in the vegetable garden.

Indoors or Outdoors

Plastic carpet runners work well inside or outside and are an inexpensive deterrent to a jumping cat, whether on your kitchen counter or your outdoor deck table. Turn the carpet runner over so that the pointy side faces up. This is not painful for your cat, but it is uncomfortable under her paws and will make her think twice before jumping up.

Odor

It may take some trial and error to determine which odors your cat finds offensive, as each cat will react differently to different smells. Remember to always check for toxicity first. If the product is safe for young children, it is generally safe for pets, but always double-check to be certain.

→   **Citrus odors are naturally offensive to cats.**

Household items: Insect repellent, colognes, muscle rubs, and aloe gel are possible deterrents.

Specialty items: Pet-safe products, available in pet stores, are designed specifically to deter your cat.

Grocery items: Orange or other citrus peels and concentrated juices generally work well, because most cats naturally do not like the smell.

Begin by protecting your carpets, floors, upholstery, and furniture from surface damage by placing weighted foil or heavy plastic at the spot you want your cat to avoid. Soak cotton balls or rags in the "smelly" substance and then place them on top of the foil or plastic. If using odors as a deterrent outdoors, you may also want to place the rags on heavy plastic to prevent the substance from soaking into the ground. Outside, the odor will lose its potency quickly and will need to be reapplied daily.

Taste

Using taste as a deterrent can be very effective, but there are a few things to consider.

- Make sure that any taste deterrent you choose is safe for people and pets.
- Some substances may damage furniture or floor finishes. Test them in a hidden location before widespread use.
- Taste deterrents developed for pets, such as Bitter Apple® or similar sprays and gels, are marketed specifically for taste aversion. Always read the instructions carefully before using.

- Insect repellents, especially those containing citronella or citrus odors, are an effective taste and odor aversive. Remember to check for toxicity.

↓ **A simple whistle can interrupt a cat's unwanted behavior.**

Noises that Startle

Items that deliver a "surprise" to startle your cat and deter her from going into an area or jumping on the countertop are available commercially, or you can create your own. These devices are meant to startle your cat, not hurt her. The information provided here is meant to help you make an informed decision prior to use.

Remote

- Put water, beans, or pebbles in an aluminum pie plate. Balance it precariously on a counter or another surface where you don't want your cat to jump. When your

DID YOU KNOW?

cat jumps on the counter, the pie plate will fall, making a loud, startling noise. After a few of these surprise encounters, your cat won't find the counter very appealing.

- Purchase a motion detector that makes a startling sound or delivers a shot of air.

Human

Use an air horn, whistle, or shaker can (a soda can filled with pennies, beans, or pebbles and taped securely shut) to get your cat's attention and interrupt her unwanted behavior.

It is important your cat does not see you using these items listed to get her attention. If your cat sees you making the noise that she hates, she will start to become afraid of you, not the items. You do not want to jeopardize your relationship with your cat, so if you cannot set up these aversives without being seen, do not use them.

↑   Provide a suitable alternative to occupy your cat.

HAPPY ENDINGS

Lexi

We already had four cats, so when my husband told me at the ARL's Pet-A-Porter fashion show that he had seen a kitten he wanted to adopt, I was a bit surprised. Being the animal lover that I am, I quickly asked him to show me the kitten. Next thing I knew, we were adopting an adorable six-month-old Scottish Fold, soon to be named Lexi. I like to joke and say that my husband "sure knows how to pick 'em," as Lexi is a wonderful, very affectionate, and playful cat. We are very happy to have her as a part of our family, and she seems to feel the same way.

—Lora

13 Training Your Cat

For those who are skeptical, yes, you can train your kitten or cat. It's just as important for felines to be properly socialized and trained as it is for their canine counterparts.

Kitten Kindergarten

We know about training classes for puppies, but what about kittens? Kitten "kindergarten" classes are geared toward kittens from eight to fifteen weeks of age, when they are most impressionable and open to learning, being trained, and bonding. Before starting classes your kitten must have documentation of a clean bill of health from the veterinarian and must have received her first set of kitten vaccinations.

Bringing your kitten to kindergarten classes allows her to interact and play with people and other kittens in a supervised setting. Assorted toys and scratching posts are part of the classroom, and a trainer will be there to initiate games to help teach the kittens proper social and play behavior. This is important, especially for kittens who were removed from their mothers and littermates too early and never had the opportunity to learn the important lesson of bite inhibition from her siblings. Kindergarten class may also introduce kittens to carriers, litter boxes, and being handled and groomed.

Kitten kindergarten should be led by a qualified instructor who has experience in cat behavior and training and uses only positive reinforcement techniques. If there is no kitten kindergarten in your area, ask your local animal shelter if they would be willing to start one up. These classes are fun for both kittens and people and are a wonderful way to give your kitten the best start on the road to being socialized, well adjusted, and happy.

Clicker Training

There are many methods of training your cat. The most humane, effective, and scientifically based training method is using a bridging stimulus commonly known as *clicker training*. Clicker training is an *operant conditioning* method used for training. In clicker training, you are using the science of learning and applying it to your cat by using a clicker as a marker for behavior.

The clicker-training method uses positive reinforcement. It is a reward-based, humane method of training. This method allows your cat to rapidly identify the behavior you desire.

↑   **Training classes aren't just for dogs—cats can learn, too!**

A clicker is a small plastic device about the size of your thumb with either a metal piece or a small button that you press, making a "click" noise. You click the clicker at the exact moment when your cat is performing the behavior you want, and immediately follow the click with a treat. The cat learns that the click means she did what you wanted and that a reward is coming; eventually, the click becomes rewarding in itself.

A cat retains tasks learned with the clicker even years after the fact and with no additional practice after the initial training. This is probably due to the fact that the animal participates fully in the learning process and applies herself to it. Interestingly, this learning retention is present in all types of positive-reinforcement training but does not regularly happen with correction-based training.

The advantage of using the clicker is that you can mark the exact behavior you want—similar to pushing the button on a camera while looking at what you want to capture in a picture. It allows you to clearly communicate the desired behavior to the cat.

The clicker is also a nonemotive sound, so your tone of voice doesn't come into play when training, which can be a huge benefit if things are not going the way you want. At first, the clicker means nothing and will have to be paired with a high-value reward.

↑ **The clicker is a small, handheld device that makes a "click" noise when you press the button.**

How to Use a Clicker

Initially, the clicker will mean nothing to your cat, so you will start off by teaching your cat that the "click" indicates a reward is coming. First, determine what motivates your cat. Treats are generally the best motivator. The treats should be small (about ¼ inch [0.5 cm]), because you will be giving multiple treats during a training session. The treats should also be soft and easy to chew, offering the cat an immediate reward.

Taking the Treat

If your cat will not take a treat from your hand, offer it to her on a plate instead. You can also throw the treat gently to your cat.

↑ **Immediately follow the click with a food reward.**

1. Find a quiet location with no distractions, if possible.
2. Have treats in one hand and the clicker in the other.
3. Click and treat right away. Do this five or six times and then stop.
4. Wait for your cat to look away and then click. If she looks back at you, you know that your clicker has meaning. If she doesn't look back at you, repeat this step. Note: This will be the one and only time you click for attention. Once you know that the clicker has meaning to the cat, you are ready to train.

How Clicker Training Works

The main principles of clicker training can be broken down into three simple steps:

1. Get the desired behavior.
2. Mark the behavior with a click.
3. Reward the behavior immediately following the click.

If you click, you *must* reward with a treat. If at any time you see your cat doing something you like, and you don't have a clicker or a treat, you still need to let her know she has done a good job. Any behavior that is rewarded is more likely to reoccur.

As you clicker train, still use a word, such as "good," to reward your cat, because over time you can fade the clicker and treats from your training and reward simply with praise.

Fear of the Click

It's important to note that some cats may be fearful of the click. Before you start, click from a distance and watch your cat's reaction. If she is afraid of the click, you may want to make a softer clicking noise with your mouth or say a short word that you do not necessarily use in conversation, such as "bing."

How Do I Teach My Cat?

There are several techniques you can use with the clicker to get the desired behavior. All of the techniques are "hands off," meaning that there is no need to grab, push, or pull your cat to teach her the things you want her to know.

Feeling Good

Some theorize that an animal's brain releases dopamine (a feel-good chemical) in response to the sound of the clicker. Think of it this way: if you really like soda, when you hear the sound of the soda can being opened, you feel that *ahhh* effect before you even take a sip.

Luring

With luring, you guide the cat into a behavior. For example, place a treat in front of the cat's nose and then move the treat up and back toward the cat's ears slowly. As the cat looks up to follow the treat with her eyes, she will lower her back end. When the cat is in a Sit position, click and treat without telling her to sit. At this point, your cat has no idea what the word "sit" means, so you want to teach the position before you put a word to it.

↑ **You can lure your cat into a Sit position by moving a treat up and back over her head.**

Repeat three or four times, using the treat but still no verbal cue. Remember to click at the exact moment she does the behavior, immediately followed by a treat. Then do it two or three times while saying "sit" so that your cat starts to make an association between the word and the action.

Next, you will work on getting the behavior without a treat in your hand. Use the same hand action you've been using, but without the treat, and say "sit." When she sits, click and treat. Now your cat knows what the word "sit" means, and you only use the treat as a reward after you click.

Targeting

Targeting is teaching your cat to touch something with some part of his body. For example, you could teach your cat to touch the tip of a pen or your finger with her

↑   **To capture the Sit, you would click and treat at the moment your kitten's rear end hits the floor.**

nose. Then, use this training to move your cat into whatever position you like. Where the head goes, the body follows. When teaching a "target," the first step is to present the target to your cat just in front of her face. She has a maximum of three seconds to touch it. If she doesn't, remove the target and place it a bit closer.

Anytime your cat touches the target within the time frame, click and treat. Once she gets the idea, start moving the target around. Teach your cat to move around to get to the target. If the cat is doing well with targeting and suddenly seems unsure, you may have moved the target too far away too soon. Break it down into smaller steps.

Capturing

To capture a behavior, watch and wait for the cat to do the desired behavior on her own. When she does, click and treat. Use this technique sparingly, and only if you cannot lure or target the desired behavior. At first, your cat won't know what she is being "clicked" for, and she could become stressed.

Training Tips

- All training sessions should be short, concise, and fun.
- Do not train to the point where your cat is bored or disinterested, or she will start to view training negatively, and you don't want that.
- If you find you are becoming frustrated or upset during a training session, end the session and try again later.
- All family members need to be consistent in training: what is allowed and not allowed, the hand motions used, the verbal cues used, and the like.

Be Proactive

Clicker training is a fantastic way to tell your cat she is doing the right thing. Unfortunately, many times, owners wait for their cat to do something wrong and then correct it. That is like letting your child run out into the road and then dragging her back and telling her it was wrong. Training is all about being *proactive*, not *reactive*. Look for the good and reward it.

Reward the Right Way

If your cat is doing something you don't like, and you interrupt her and cue her to do something you do like, wait about three to five seconds before rewarding the desirable behavior. You don't want her to think you are rewarding her for both the undesirable and desirable behaviors.

- Try not to teach too many behaviors at once. Focus on teaching the basic behaviors well before moving on to more complex exercises.
- Teach your cat the desirable behaviors you want—don't just expect her to know how to behave.
- If your cat does not perform a given behavior when you give the cue, spend some more time working on that behavior so she knows it well.
- Practice.
- Remember that every time you interact with your cat, you are teaching her something. Try to make sure that each interaction is an appropriate one.
- Finish each session while the cat still wants more, keeping in mind that some cats have short attention spans, are easily distracted, or are easily fatigued.

14 Keeping Your Cat Safe Indoors and Out

There is a long-running debate on whether cats should live indoors, outdoors, or a combination of both. The simple fact is that indoor cats live much longer than outdoor cats. The dangers to your cat that exist outdoors do not exist inside the house.

Can a cat that has lived outside live happily indoors? The ARL takes in thousands of "outside strays" every year and then adopts these cats out with the idea that they will be house cats. The ease by which outdoor cats can be confined to their homes without any problems makes me believe that cats can easily live indoors as part of the family. There is no reason to let your cat outside to annoy neighbors or risk her safety.

Cat Facts

The average life expectancy of an indoor cat is sixteen years or longer. A cat that lives exclusively outside lives an average of three to five years.

↑　**Give your indoor cat entertaining views of the outdoors.**

Indoors

Your cat can live indoors happily. Your cat's "wanting-to-go-outside" feeling will fade away if you make the indoors a fun and comforting place for her. Take these steps to make the inside as desirable as the outside.

- Set up bird feeders outside your cat's favorite window so she gets the mental stimulation of the outdoors.
- Grow some cat grass in an inside planter so she can still "eat" grass.
- Make sure there are sunny spots where your cat can lie down.
- Have a lot of different cat toys for her to play with inside the house.
- Adopt another cat so she has a cat friend.
- Open windows that will allow the smells of the outdoors to come in but will not allow your cat to escape.

Once your cat has everything she really needs indoors, she will stop going to the door to be let out after a few weeks.

Safety in the House

- Loose screens: Make sure that your window screens are securely in place so your cat cannot accidentally fall out a window.

- Toilet cleaner and toilets: Keep toilet lids closed so your cat or kitten doesn't jump up and into the toilet, especially if you use a cleaner that is automatically dispensed into your bowl upon flushing.

- Sharp objects: Be careful not to leave sharp objects, such as knives or scissors, on counters in case your cat decides to explore.

- Hot stoves: Do not leave your cat alone in the kitchen if the stovetop is hot. If she jumps onto the stovetop while it is hot, she will not have time to react before the pads of her feet suffer burns.

Outdoors

Despite the saying that cats have nine lives, they really don't. They do not know that they should stay out of the street or how to avoid being hit by a car. As much as we would like, we really can't teach our cat to stay in the yard. If you feel you must allow your cat outside time, follow these suggestions to help keep her as safe as possible.

↑ A cat patio, or "catio," is a secure outdoor play area for a cat.

↑ Most cats can easily scale fences and escape fenced yards.

In the yard: Use a cat collar and correctly fitted harness. You should always supervise your cat while on a harness so she doesn't get entangled or injured on a fence or other outdoor hazard. The collar and harness is a way to let your cat be outside with you while staying secure in the yard.

On the deck: Do not put your cat on a collar and tether on an elevated deck. If she can reach the edge, she could accidentally step over the edge and hang herself. This is another reason your cat should always be supervised outdoors.

Fenced-in yards: Do not assume that a fence will contain your cat. Even cats that have been declawed may still be able to scale 6-foot (2-meter) wooden fences and take off for a romp around the neighborhood.

Remember, just because you used to let your cat outside, it doesn't mean that you should continue to do so. Start keeping her inside. With patience and a short period of adjustment, your cat will live happily and safely in the house with you.

Finding Your Lost Housecat

If your indoor cat slips through a door or falls through a loose window screen and gets out, you need to know what to do to bring her safely back home. It is important to remember that most housecats who escape actually stay near their own homes and yards. Many people assume that if a cat runs out a door, she will keep on running, but that is typically not the case at all. A panicked cat will often stay alongside her home for some comfort, so look under a deck, in the bushes, in an open garage, under the hood of your car, and the like. Be sure to look up in case your cat climbed a tree in your yard.

↑ Outdoor hiding places can be dangerous to cats.

↑ With a collar and ID tag, your cat will be identified as someone's pet rather than a stray.

If you don't find your cat in your yard, notify your neighbors that she is missing. Ask for permission to look in and around their yards and garages and ask them to check under the hoods of their cars. Remind them to keep their eyes open and to let their children know to look out for the cat when they are playing outside. Make sure that neighbors have your phone number to get in touch with you right away if they see your cat. Offer a reward.

If you don't find her nearby, do the following:

- Make flyers and post them in at least a five-block radius of your home. Be sure to include a photo of the cat, your contact information, and that you are offering a reward to anyone who finds your cat.
- Notify local animal shelters, animal-control agencies, and law-enforcement agencies that your cat is lost and that you are looking for her. Give them some flyers. Tell them to contact you if they find your cat, dead or alive.
- Inquire at local veterinarians' offices and emergency animal clinics. Someone may have found your cat, injured or not, and taken her to a nearby veterinarian or clinic for care and safety. Leave flyers at these offices.

- Make "lost pet" posts to your social media accounts and online to community forums and any lost pet boards. Also check for any messages that a cat has been found.
- Put a "lost pet" ad in your local newspaper for those who are not online. Run it for at least two weeks.
- Set humane traps around your yard and in your garage (leave the garage door open a crack) with the food that your cat normally eats. Use a camera, such as a security camera, on the trap to see if your cat is coming near the traps.
- If you have other cats in the home, place a used litter box near your door so that the lost cat can smell her housemates.
- Put a food bowl on your porch or by your front door and use a baby monitor to see or hear if your cat is coming near the food.

Whatever you do, don't give up. We know of many cases where a cat was gone for days or longer, only to return. Keep at it. It can be tiring, but exhaust all avenues and follow all tips to find your cat.

Dealing with Free-Roaming Cats

Look around any animal shelter, and you will see "stray" listed as the reason many cats are there. A stray is often a free-roaming cat that a kind human found and took to the shelter for care and, hopefully, adoption.

You may find it surprising that many free-roaming cats are actually very domesticated and sweet—even those that need to be humanely trapped because they initially won't let people get close to them. Other stray cats may be domestic cats that have returned to a semiwild state, who were never kept as pets or are feral in nature. These cats are very difficult for an animal shelter to place into homes. They can, however, be part of a spayed/neutered cat colony that is returned to the same area as long as there is a caretaker to provide food, water, shelter, and medical attention when necessary.

↑ **Even cat lovers may not appreciate stray cats in their yards and gardens.**

Problems and Solutions

Outdoor, or free-roaming, cats can cause problems for you and your neighbors.

- Using yards, gardens, or sandboxes as a litter box
- Getting into garages or other buildings
- Chasing away birds from feeders
- Walking on cars and leaving pawprints
- Getting into garbage cans

↑ Protect birds from free-roaming cats with items made to deter squirrels.

The ARL often gets calls from people asking how to deal with free-roaming cats. People don't want to hurt the cats and don't blame them for looking for food or using their gardens as a litter box, but they want the cats to leave their yards, cars, birds, and property alone. We of course advise them how to deal with these issues using humane methods, such as positive reinforcement.

Determine if the cat is a stray or someone's pet. Of course, the ideal solution is for all cat owners to keep their cats safely indoors. If you know where the cat lives, ask the owner to keep the cat inside. If the cat has no owner, then she needs to be taken somewhere safe, such as an animal shelter, where she can be indoors and properly cared for. A shelter can spay/neuter cats so that they aren't reproducing in a world already overpopulated by cats.

Use natural deterrents, such as odor, texture, and movement. Yelling out your door to get the

↑ **Sprinklers can deter cats from hanging out on your lawn.**

cat out of the garden is not going to work. The cat will be afraid of you and will not understand that you simply want her out of your garden. She will only learn not to visit when you are around.

- Odor: Cats, in general, dislike the smell of citrus. Place oranges or safe orange scent around the area you want the cat to stay away from. The cat will associate the this area with the citrus smell and move on.
- Texture: A plastic carpet runner turned upside down on the hood of your car will create an uncomfortable resting place for a cat. Keep it there for a few weeks, and the cat will decide that the hood of your car is not a good bed or sunning spot. The plastic carpet runner, pointed side up, can also be used around your garden to make an unpleasant walking and digging surface.
- Movement: A motion-detector sprinkler systems in the yard is a very effective deterrent. The cat will be startled and a little wet but will remain unharmed.

No Poison!

Never put out or use poison. Not only is it inhumane and unnecessary, but you could poison other animals or even children by mistake. Plus, it will only take care of one cat and not keep other cats away.

Cat Facts

- A fertile cat can produce one or two litters per year, with four to six kittens per litter.

- It is impossible to determine how many stray cats live in the United States, but estimates range up to 70 million.

- In approximately seven years, one unspayed female cat and one unneutered male cat and their offspring could result in more than 400,000 kittens!

Additionally, implement the following practices to make your yard less appealing for cats:

- Hang bird feeders up high or in areas a cat cannot reach. Do not put feeders on your deck railing or on the ground. Safe products are available to keep squirrels from climbing up to bird feeders, and these products will also deter cats.
- Keep lids on garbage cans and close garage doors. Cats are extremely curious. Exploring buildings and sifting through garbage cans is a natural instinct for them.
- There are commercial products on the market to repel cats. These products have been deemed safe by the EPA. Check with your local pet- or garden-supply store for more information on these products.

Humanely Trapping a Free-Roaming Cat

Option 1: See if the cat is friendly enough to let you pick her up. Offer the cat some food and see if she will come to you to get it. If so, it is a good sign that you will at some point be able to earn her trust and she will let you pick her up. Be patient, as the process can be slow and methodical and require some time. Have a cat carrier handy so you can put her into the carrier immediately.

Option 2: Buy a humane trap at a hardware or pet-supply store. Additionally, animal-control agencies often will loan or rent these types of traps. A humane trap should have food and water set up in it. Ideally, the cat will enter the trap to get the food and trigger the door to close, leaving the cat inside. If you choose to use a trap, make sure you are available to check it often so that a cat is not trapped inside without water or in harsh weather. Never trap a cat and take her somewhere else to let her go. Leave the cat in the trap and take her to an animal shelter or contact a local trap-neuter-return (TNR) program. (See page 152.)

Humane Live-Trapping

Q: Two cats were dumped at my house in the country. I have been trying to get closer to them by softly meowing and offering food. I have been doing this for a few weeks but to no avail. I am starting to worry about the cats' safety because they are outside all the time.

A: We decided to try humane live traps, and the homeowner was able to catch both cats within two days. She brought the cats to the ARL. After getting them out of the traps, we found that both of them were very sweet and loving. Both were placed for adoption after the appropriate hold time, and they both found forever homes. Follow-up showed both cats to be sweet, affectionate indoor family members who had learned to use their litter boxes.

↑ You may be able to borrow a humane trap from a local animal-control agency or shelter.

↑   Feral cats often live in colonies on the streets.

Feral Cats

You don't typically see feral cats up for adoption at your local animal shelter. There is a lot of confusion as to what a feral cat is. When we get calls from the public, asking for help with cat behavior issues, people sometimes say their cat is wild and feral. When we start to inquire where the cat stays and sleeps, and if she is good with other pets and kids, we discover that the cat just has bad manners or needs a playmate.

Feral cats are described as the offspring of stray cats that are not spayed or neutered. They are wild in the sense that they are not used to human touch or interaction. Most of the time, they have to be live-trapped to be moved or brought into the shelter because they won't allow themselves to be caught by people. They are like wild animals that want to avoid humans.

Feral female cats can become pregnant at as early as five months of age and can give birth up to three times in a year. All of these pregnancies starting at an early age are stressful on these adult feral cats. Their kittens, if they live on the streets, will be feral as well. More than half of these kittens are likely to die without human intervention.

Males who roam and fight to find mates and defend their territories may be injured and transmit diseases to one another through bite wounds. They may also live in pain because of these wounds.

Feral cats deserve compassion and understanding and to be cared for as much as the cats that share our homes and lives. Feral cats and their offspring are often victims of abandonment or being born in the wild. The life they know is simply trying to survive on the streets.

Adult feral cats do not typically adapt to living as pets in someone's home. Success is possible with kittens if they are taken in early enough. They need to be constantly handled and socialized, and they must be introduced to socialization almost immediately after birth.

Feral cats tend to group up and live in colonies. Generally, they are all related, and the colony will occupy and defend the area in which they live. For example, they may find a restaurant where they can find scraps in the garbage, or a kindhearted person who puts food out for them. The colony will claim that spot and keep it clear of others. Interestingly enough, humans in the area may not even realize the cats are there because they do all they can to avoid human interaction and become experts at staying hidden.

↑   The tip of the cat's left ear has been clipped to indicate that she has been trapped, neutered, and returned.

↑ Some cat colonies have human caretakers who provide food, water, and possibly even veterinary care.

Trap-Neuter-Return Programs (TNR)

Some people and communities are strongly against feral cat colonies, even if those colonies are being cared for under a trap-neuter-rReturn (TNR) program. They may feel that wildlife is endangered by these feral cats. In any case, the cat population in the United States is bursting at the seams, and there is a growing need across the country for community-wide TNR programs.

TNR is a nonlethal program, of which spaying and neutering is a main piece. If implemented correctly, TNR prevents more and more cats from being born into a very tough existence on the streets. TNR programs also ensure the care of these cats and improve their health and quality of life.

Overall, many feral cats don't survive. If they do survive, their lives are not easy without human caretakers. If you have feral cats in your area, get involved. TNR programs do work and can be a solution for many urban and rural situations. Visit Alleycat Allies at *www.alleycat.org* to learn more and find how to start a program in your area.

HAPPY ENDINGS

Sweetie Pie

I volunteer with cats at the ARL and had been keeping an eye out for a special guy. I tell everyone that Sweetie chose me. The first time I petted him, he turned belly up and licked my nose. I knew then that he was the one for me and my husband.

Because he was found as a stray, we didn't know much about Sweetie's history. We could tell that he had always been an outdoor cat, so we weren't sure how well he would adjust to being cooped up in our apartment. As it turns out, he prefers it! He appreciates being safe from the elements.

Sweetie likes his life as king of the great indoors. I have to watch where I step because he will sleep sprawled out, belly up, with a big cat grin on his face. He has learned to enjoy, even demand, laps. He will wrap his front paws around my leg, rest his chin on my knee, and heave a sigh of pure contentment. Then he falls asleep—and so do my legs, because he weighs more than 16 pounds (7.25 kg).

We love Sweetie Pie and consider ourselves lucky to have found him. He truly is our forever friend.

—Deirdre and Chris

15 Dealing with Aggression

All animals, including cats, display aggression. It is a natural behavior. Cats use aggression for survival or to ward off perceived threats. Aggression can be directed at people, other cats, or other animals. Unfortunately, if it is unprovoked or seems inappropriate, it is not a behavior you want in your pet. Aggression displays in cats range from hissing to violent attacks. All aggressive displays should be taken seriously.

Most aggressive displays are due to your cat being defensive. There are very few animals in the world that attack without provocation. There are many types of aggression, and a correct diagnosis from a veterinarian, veterinary behaviorist, or animal behavior specialist, is paramount. On that note, it is important to understand that the information provided here on aggression does not replace a consultation with a behavior professional.

Seek Help

Aggression is necessary for survival, but when that aggression is misplaced or excessive and causes harm to you or other animals, it is not acceptable. Aggression is a serious issue, and you should seek help immediately at the first signs of any aggressive behavior.

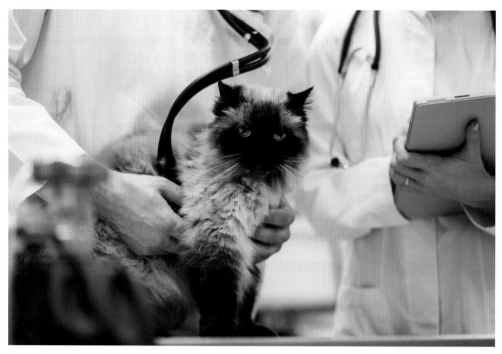

↑ A veterinary checkup is your first step in diagnosing or eliminating causes of agression.

Diagnosing and Treating Aggression

In some cases, medical conditions can contribute to aggression. Your cat should have a thorough physical examination and blood analysis within three months of a behavior consultation. This is needed to rule out any medical condition that may be contributing to the problem behavior. A behavior consultation will help determine in what circumstances the pet is aggressive and whether the aggression is toward family members, strangers, other pets in the household, or strange pets.

Keeping a diary is the best way to ensure an accurate record of aggressive displays. This will also help determine if treatment is working to decrease the occurrences of aggression. Behavior modification techniques or changes to the pet's environment may be necessary to modify aggression problems.

Types of Aggression

Fear Aggression

Fear aggression arises when a cat is exposed and reacts to a perceived threat or stimuli. Situations previously associated with an unpleasant experience can also trigger fear aggression. Many cats may try to escape the area, hide, or climb up high where it is safe when they are fearful. If prevented from escaping because they are cornered, they are likely to fight.

The best way to approach a fearful cat is in a calm, confident, and friendly manner. This is likely to be met with a less fearful response. Fear aggression toward family members might arise out of punishment or other unpleasant experiences associated with them; it is best to avoid verbal or physical correction.

Play Aggression

Play aggression could be a contradiction in terms. When your cat or kitten is playing, he is having fun, and his body language would not be that of a defensive cat. He may grab, bite, and chase, but these behaviors can be redirected into more appropriate ones. (See Chapter 8.)

↑   **Aggressive behavior shown in play is still inappropriate.**

Territorial Aggression

Territorial aggression is usually exhibited toward other cats that approach or reside on your property. This can happen when you bring another cat into the house, or when cats have been living together quite happily and one reaches social maturity at one to two years of age. These sudden changes may cause fear or anxiety. It can also be directed at people or other animals.

Pain-Induced Aggression

When you are in pain, the last thing you want is anyone to touch you where you hurt. Even if your cat is not exhibiting pain, certain medical conditions may make him more irritable and prone to aggression. Fear and anxiety further compound many of these cases. Unfortunately, once your cat learns that aggression is successful in making you go away, it may recur when similar situations arise in the future, whether or not the pain is still present.

↑ Aggression among outdoor cats is usually territorial in nature.

Maternal Aggression

Maternal aggression occurs when a cat is protecting her babies. This can be modified by using desensitization and counterconditioning techniques along with highly motivating rewards.

Redirected Aggression

Redirected aggression arises out of other forms of aggression and is defined by the cat taking her aggression out on something or someone other than the actual target of her aggression. She may take her aggression out on what or whom she can get to: possibly you or another cat or pet in the home.

In this case, it is important to identify, treat, and prevent exposure to the real trigger of the aggression. An aggressive reaction is likely to occur when the cat is aroused at the same time that you or another pet is approaching. You must avoid a highly aroused cat until she calms down.

Petting-Induced Aggression

Some cats bite while being petted, while others are intolerant of all handling. Most cats with petting aggression accept a certain amount of petting but then become highly agitated and attack when they have had enough. This can be difficult to understand, because many of these cats seek attention and seem to enjoy physical contact from the owner for a while. It seems that they have a certain threshold for the amount of physical interaction they can tolerate.

First, identify and avoid responses that might increase your cat's fear or anxiety. Make all handling experiences positive. When handling your cat, do not physically restrain her; cats that are placed in positions where they feel constrained or unable to escape might become aggressive.

Social-Status Aggression

The social structure of and relationship between cats is continually being researched. Cats do maintain social relationships when living in groups, leading to the speculation that they do have some form of social structure. They may maintain this social structure through aggressive displays and actions. Assertive behavior—such as soliciting attention through attacks or biting, aggression during petting, attempts to control the environment by blocking access to doorways, refusing to be moved from sleeping areas, stalking family members, and showing threatening or aggressive behavior to owners passing by— may be displays of social status. Some cats may show aggression toward their owners or other cats when protecting their resources, such as a favorite toy, a sleeping place, or even you.

Because cats are known to be a social species, it is not surprising that some cats will assert their authority or leadership when challenged by a subordinate cat or a family member in the home. When a cat in the household dies, there will be a shift in the social standings as the cats adjust and reset the rules of who has what. You may even find that a once-shy cat steps up and claims something for which he previously was not strong enough to challenge another cat.

↖ **A hierarchy is established between multiple cats in a home.**

Guarding Food

Mick says: I have a cat who will continually force any one of my four other cats away from the dry food bowl when he hears another cat eating, So I now have five food bowls placed around my home, including one inside a cat tree. When a cat is eating there, her rear end blocks the entrance to the cat tree, so my resource-guarding cat can't get to the bowl. Also, with five bowls, there are too many to guard all at once, so he gives up. This same cat will defer and walk away from all of the other cats, including our kitten, if I put down wet food.

Learned Aggression

When a cat learns that aggressive behavior can be rewarding (i.e., successful at removing a perceived threat), it is likely that her aggression will reoccur or escalate. Sometimes owners inadvertently reward certain forms of aggression when, in attempts to calm their pets and reduce aggression, they actually encourage the behavior with petting or verbal reassurances. Cats that are threatened or punished for aggressive displays may become even more aggressive as well.

Resource Guarding

Resource guarding is exactly what it sounds like: "I will defend something I find valuable." This may be as simple as pushing another cat away from a food bowl. The other cat defers, because it is not as important to the second cat as it is to the first. Unfortunately, some of these situations may turn into full-blown fights. It depends on the cats involved.

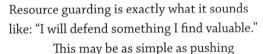

16 Special-Needs and Elderly Cats

Living with cats that are deaf or blind may seem to be challenging, but they are quite capable of living happy, normal lives. Your cat may also face challenges as she gets older, but you can help your senior cat enjoy her golden years with you.

Deaf Cats

Deaf cats should always be kept inside. They are not able to hear cars coming or other dangers. Deaf cats hear in their own way. They have an extraordinary ability to feel the vibrations from walking, other animals, or sounds such as an oven door closing or furniture being moved. Sometimes, because of this extraordinary ability, you may start to question if the cat is really deaf. Some deaf cats are easily startled. If you have a deaf cat that startles easily, you may want to stomp on the floor to let the cat know you are coming.

Interestingly, deaf cats are sometimes the most vocal. Some deaf cats, however, do not meow at all and are very quiet. Others meow loudly when playing or when they see a bird or something else outside.

All cats have a need to be high in the air, but this need is more extreme for deaf cats. It is likely a

DID YOU KNOW?

If your cat is deaf, her ears will still flicker and move—perhaps because of the vibrations she feels, or perhaps it may be a way for her to communicate with her humans and other pets in the house.

↑ **Being up high, with a view of her surroundings, is a security need for a deaf cat.**

security issue. A deaf cat wants to be able to see what is coming her way because she cannot hear it. Be sure to give a deaf cat places where she can be up high, such as a scratching post, a dresser, or a shelf in a closet.

DID YOU KNOW?

Your deaf cat understands affection solely by feel, as opposed to also hearing your words. Pet your deaf cat as you would any other cat.

Communicate with your deaf cat by learning some basic sign language or making up your own hand motions. You can teach him cues by sign, such as "come," "get off the counter," and "no." Mouthing the words clearly at the same time reinforces your message. Of course, your own body language and facial expressions will go a long way in telling him what you wish to communicate.

With this in mind, you need to provide a little more care with a deaf cat. For example, a hearing cat may jump up on a counter near the hot stove and you can easily shout "no!" or "get down!" to her, and she will respond. With a deaf cat, you need to train her not to get on the counter near the hot stove to begin with, because she won't hear your shouts of concern.

Blind Cats

If the owner takes care to provide a safe, stimulating environment, a blind cat or kitten can have a happy life. Because blind cats are often able to adapt very well, many owners do not realize that their cats are blind for a considerable length of time.

The degree of blindness in cats varies from total to partial blindness (cloudy sight, ability to differentiate between light and shade, tunnel vision). This is similar to the way human blindness varies. With most cats, especially as they age, the loss of sight is gradual, so cats are able to adapt gradually. When a cat becomes blind suddenly, it is noticeable to the owners, because the cat may bump into things when she walks or may meow more often because she is confused.

Your cat may develop different behaviors until she learns to adjust. She may strike out in self-defense at sudden movements or at being touched or startled suddenly. Your cat may not want to leave one particular spot, like her sleeping area. She may stop using her litter box because she doesn't want to move from the spot she knows. Blind cats tend to meow or vocalize more because they need to know that their owners are near and need to be reassured.

Blind cats rely on scent and memory to find their way around, so keep furniture in the same places and do not leave obstacles in unexpected places. If your cat is

↑ **A cat with one eye lacks normal depth perception and will need special considerations.**

↑ **You may think that carrying your blind cat is helpful, but it actually can disorient her.**

prone to bumping into furniture, try padding table and chair legs with old pillows or foam to reduce impact damage. While most blind cats soon memorize routes, not all manage this feat and instead rely on bumping into their signposts. Whiskers become more important to blind cats to judge their proximity to objects. Fully blind cats may clamber onto things rather than jump, but many also memorize heights and distances. Don't put a blind cat onto raised surfaces, because she will probably be disoriented and fall off.

Do not carry a blind cat around. This can disorient her, so if you must move her, place her somewhere she knows well, such as her feeding or sleeping area so she can easily get her bearings. Don't move her litter box or feeding areas, because she needs to be able to find them easily by memory. She may actually even use these familiar places as markers to know where something else is in relation.

Sound is also important to a blind cat. Noisy toys, such as those with bells inside them, paper sacks, or scrunched-up paper balls, will provide stimulation and become sounds she enjoys.

Do not allow a blind cat outdoors to roam. If she is allowed to roam freely and is chased by another animal, she may become lost or run into the path of traffic. Because she relies so much on scent and sound, a lost blind cat will probably be unable to find her way home once she is beyond her normal territory. Make sure that your cat is wearing a collar at all times with an identification tag that states her address and disability, in case she escapes. She should also be microchipped. Remember, the best approach is to never let your blind cat outside.

Elderly Cats

As your cat gets older, she will need a little extra attention. Make regular twice-yearly appointments with your veterinarian for checkups, including having her teeth checked and her weight recorded. Talk to your veterinarian about any changing nutrition needs to make sure you are giving her the right food for her age.

↑   **Give your senior cat the love and attention that she's used to.**

Continue to provide enrichment for your senior cat. Interactive toys keep your cat's mind active and healthy, and they will provide some physical exercise as well. Also continue to give your cat the attention that she needs. An emotionally happy cat is a healthier cat.

Consider if your older cat needs changes in her litter box. Cats may develop arthritis as they get older, and if this is the case for your cat, she may benefit from a litter box with lower sides for easier access. Likewise, she may need help to get up on your bed or the couch to be near you. You can purchase "pet steps" at a pet-supply store that your cat can use to climb up and down instead of jumping on and off the furniture. Also provide your cat with a soft bed or another comfortable place for her to curl up and sleep on the floor.

Make sure that your cat's litter box and food/water bowls are in locations that are easy for her to get to. If your cat can no longer go up and down the basement stairs, move the litter box and bowls to the first floor.

HAPPY ENDINGS

Brody

I convinced my husband to stop by the ARL so we could see the new shelter. Even though I desperately wanted a cat, I promised my husband that I only wanted to look and would not ask to bring a cat home. Well, we fell in love with Brody, a four-year-old, front-declawed male that had been picked up as a stray, and we brought him home with us.

It only took Brody a couple of days to settle in. By the end of the first week, he was jumping up on our bed at night and lying between us, just purring away. Since we do not have any children, Brody has his own bedroom with an attached bathroom. When we have house guests, they stay in "Brody's room."

Brody was the poster child for a perfect first cat. Then, about six months after we adopted him, I caught him spraying on a wall. A good friend suggested I take him to the vet to rule out a medical condition, because spraying can often be a symptom of a urinary infection.

It turned out that Brody did have an infection, and the vet put him on antibiotics. When the antibiotics didn't work, an X-ray revealed a bladder stone the size of an olive. The poor guy had been suffering for months. Brody was such a tough cat that, despite the pain, he never cried out when urinating or exhibited any other symptoms of having a stone.

After surgery to remove the stone, Brody was put on a special diet to prevent any future stones. We feel blessed to have Brody. He was placed with us for a reason. Not every pet owner can afford surgery or special food. Luckily, we can, and today Brody is a very happy and healthy cat.

My husband and I have jobs that can be stressful. Yet all that stress goes away when we come home at the end of the day and Brody is waiting. When he hears the garage door, he comes to the back door to wait for us. He sits between the blinds and the glass, meowing at us.

We are grateful for the work of the ARL and all animal shelters. I wish there were no need for shelters, but as long as they exist, I will continue to support them. Thank you for providing our house with such an amazing cat—he makes it a real home.

—Mickie

17 Other Situations

Cats and Babies

Cats and babies can be a great combination. Despite what a lot of people believe, cats are social animals and love "their" people. When a new baby is coming into the family, there are things you can do to prepare your cat. It is important to remember that babies and cats should never be left alone or unsupervised.

Before Baby Comes Home

Set up the nursery early and let your cat explore the room. *Never* allow the cat in the crib. The best way to ensure that the cat stays out of the crib is with a crib cover. You can also make the inside of the crib unattractive to the cat by filling it with cans of coins. When the cans move, they will make a loud noise, thereby making the crib an unattractive place for a cat.

Replace the regular door of the baby's room with a screen door. This allows you to have the door shut, but because it is a screen, your cat won't feel left out while you are in the room, tending to the baby. It also serves as a way to see inside the baby's room while keeping the cat out.

Purchase lotions and bath products that you will be using for your baby. Leave them out and open to get your cat used to some of the "baby smells." Put some of the baby lotion on you and others in the household so the cat gets used to his owners having this scent on them.

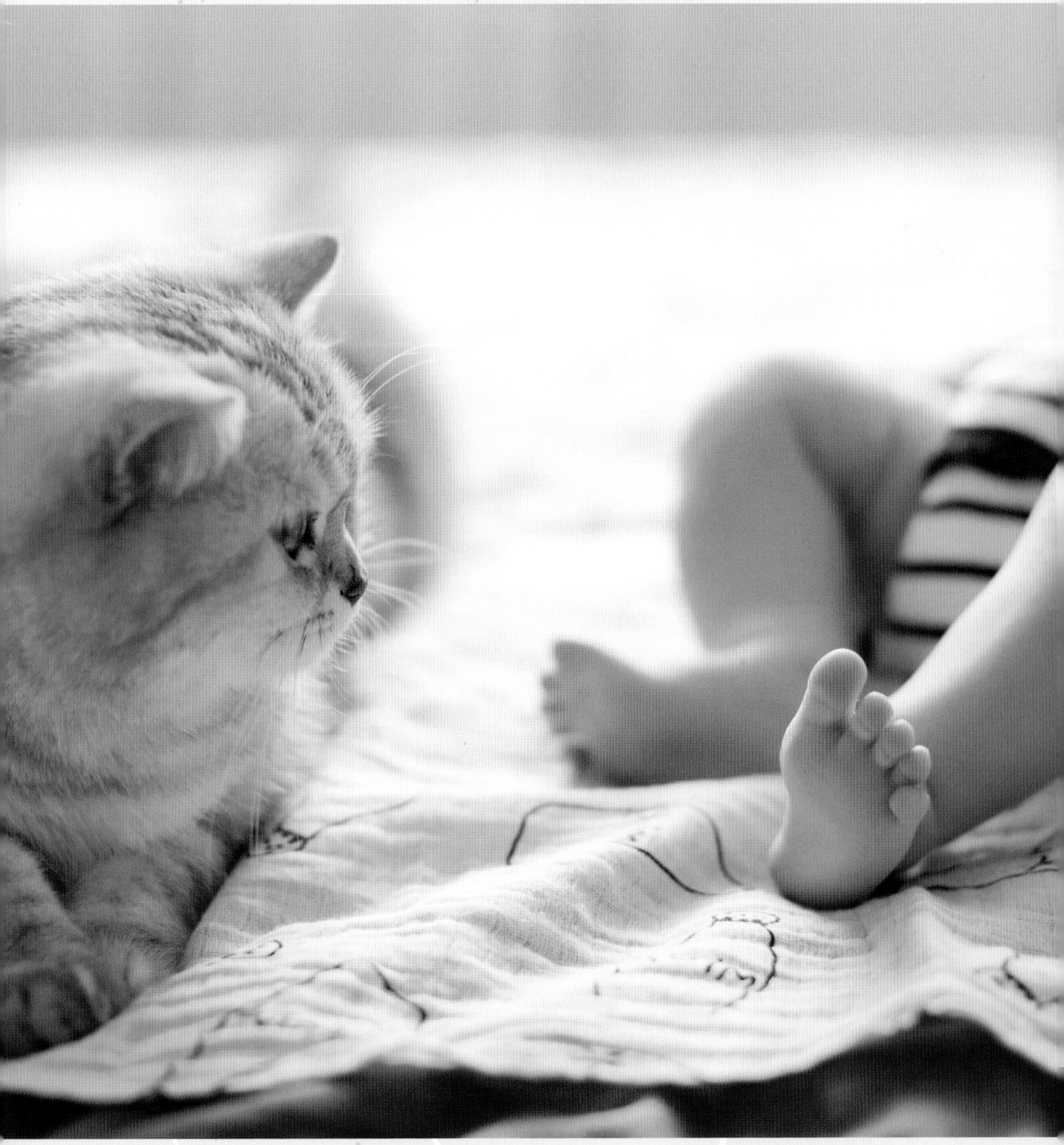

↑ **A screen door on the baby's room will help prevent the cat from feeling left out.**

Plan early and start setting aside time to play with your cat. For example, if, after the baby is born, you anticipate being able to play and spend one-on-one time with your cat in the morning before the baby gets up and at night after the baby goes to sleep, start spending ten or so minutes playing with your cat during those times. This will get your cat prepared for "her time" with you. Don't overcompensate before the baby comes and play with the cat all the time. Once the baby is born, you won't have that kind of time, and the cat won't get the attention she was used to.

Cats need many toys. Make sure that your cat has lots of toys that she can play with when you are busy. Remember, do not ever use your fingers or feet to play with your cat! (See Chapter 7 for more about toys.)

Place your cat's litter box and food and water bowls where they will remain after the baby comes home. Locate them in places that a crawling baby cannot get to. This way, your cat can maintain his territory and not feel invaded.

Tape the sound of a baby crying and start playing it off and on to familiarize your cat with the sounds. Vary the times of day and night you play it so the cat gets used to hearing the sounds at any time.

↑ **Give your cat a variety of toys to play with so she won't be bored while you're caring for the baby.**

Buy a toy doll that crawls and have it crawl around your house. Reward the cat with treats or praise when the cat interacts appropriately with the toy doll. Do not punish the cat if she reacts badly; just remove the doll and try it again until she demonstrates appropriate behavior. Hold, rock, and carry the doll as you would a baby. When the baby comes home, these actions will be familiar to your cat.

When Baby Comes Home

After the baby comes home, there are many things you can do to ease the transition for your cat.

- When visitors come to the house, have them pay attention to the baby and the cat if the cat wants attention.
- When the cat is in the room with the baby, give the cat treats and special attention.
- Spend some one-on-one time with your cat.
- Try not to change your cat's routine.
- When the baby starts to crawl, walk, or express an interest in the cat, teach your child not to poke at the cat or pull her tail.

↑ For everyone's safety, always supervise interactions between the baby and the cat.

Cats and Carriers

Getting a cat used to a cat carrier can be a challenge. Your cat rarely leaves the safety of her home except to go to the veterinarian's office, but it is a good idea to get your cat used to being in a carrier, at least for these trips to the vet. Additionally, you may need to travel or move with your cat, so having her as calm as possible in the carrier is good for both of you.

Positive Reinforcement

You want to reward the cat with the things she likes whenever the baby is around. Do not punish the cat for inappropriate behavior, just remove the cat or the baby from the room. If you punish the cat, she will associate being punished with the baby, and it will take her longer to accept the baby.

To get started, set the carrier out with the door open. Let your cat sniff and inspect the carrier. Say "good cat" and walk away. All is good when the carrier is out in the house. Do not push your cat into the carrier; just let her be around it and inspect it. Add treats to the carrier. Let the cat sniff and find the treats and walk into the carrier to get them. Make them extra-good treats—something your cat can't refuse.

After a couple of weeks, if the cat has shown interest and gone into the carrier to get the treats, start putting the cat in the carrier and shutting the door. Put a favorite toy and towel in the crate so it is soft and comfortable. Leave the cat in there with treats for a few minutes and then open the door. While the cat is in there, say "good kitty" in a happy voice. You are making the carrier a happy place for the cat. The cat gets to go in and get tasty treats, hear praise, and then come out. All is good in the cat's world. Do this for a week or two.

Next, take the cat in the carrier for a very short car ride, just out of and back into the driveway. Take the carrier and cat back into the house and let your cat out of the carrier. Gradually lengthen the time the cat is in the carrier and traveling in the car.

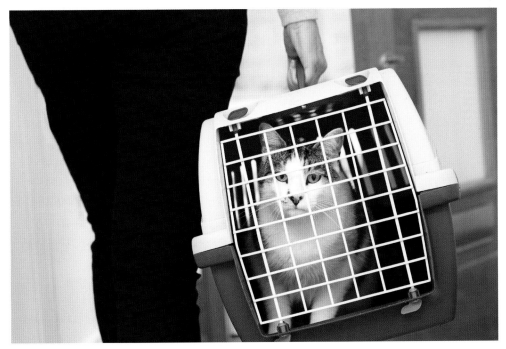

↑ **Your cat needs to be acclimated to a carrier, even if you only need to use it infrequently.**

↑ **Secure in her carrier is the only safe way for your cat to travel.**

You are showing her that being in the carrier and in the car doesn't necessarily mean a trip to the vet.

Continue with treats while your cat is in the carrier and when she gets home and you let her out of the carrier. All of her short stays in the carrier and trips in the car result in good things for her, such as treats and praise. Over time, your cat will start to look at the carrier and car rides as OK things. When you have to take your cat to the veterinarian, provide treats while at the veterinarian's office as well. You are making even the trip to the veterinarian a good thing.

When taking your cat out of the carrier, it is best to open the door and let the cat walk out on her own. If she won't come out, gently reach in while talking to your cat and bring her out. Remember to open the door to the carrier only when your cat is safely in your house or the veterinarian's office. Cats can get stressed, so opening the door to the carrier outside or in a room that is not secured is not safe for your cat.

Traveling with Your Cat

Ensure the safety and well-being of your cat when traveling. Never travel with your cat loose in the car. A cat can get under your feet or climb on you and cause your vision or movement to be impaired. Be sure to travel with your cat safely confined. For short distances, use a cat carrier. For longer distances, use a large dog crate and include a litter box, cat bed, toys, food, and water. (See Moving to a New Home on page 179 for tips on traveling long distances with your cat.) Never open the crate door until you have the cat secured inside a house or room indoors.

Keep in mind that traveling is stressful on a cat, and opening the crate door in an unsecured car or room could result in your cat escaping out onto the road or unfamiliar territory. Have a breakaway collar and tags on your cat, along with a cat harness. Reach into the kennel and clip a leash onto the harness before you open the door. This way, you will have control of your cat the minute you open the door. Do not leave the leash on the cat in the carrier. You do not want your cat to get tangled in it.

DID YOU KNOW?

Studies show that classical music has a calming effect on cats, so play classical music and talk to your cat during trips in the car.

↑ **Never let your cat loose in the car. She could be injured or distract the driver, both of which are dangerous.**

Traveling Tips

- Have current photos of your cat from different angles so you can use them if she does escape.
- Be sure that all of your cat's vaccinations are current before traveling, and have your cat's medical records with you.
- Have your cat microchipped. A microchip is a permanent form of identification. Be sure to have your microchip registered so that the microchip company can contact you if your cat is found and her microchip scanned.
- If your cat is taking medication, bring it with you. Include some extra days' worth of medication just in case you are delayed from returning home as planned.
- Take your cat's food with you so she can stay on the same diet. Take extra food, and don't forget to bring treats for positive reinforcement.
- Put a T-shirt or other item that smells like you in the crate with the cat when traveling.
- If your cat has a favorite toy, take it along.

↑ **Whether a road trip or a trip to the vet, your cat will be safe in her carrier.**

Help for Your Stressed Cat

Feliway® is a synthetic copy of the feline facial pheromone used by cats to mark their territory as safe and secure. It is not a drug, so it doesn't have the potential side effects that drugs might. It is used with cats that are stressed or to help with aggression and spraying.

Moving to a New Home

Whether you are moving to another home in the same city or relocating to another state, a move can be stressful on your cat. Cats are creatures of habit that like their lives with as little disruption as possible. Cats react to changes in their surroundings at different levels. One cat may wonder what's going on and be curious about all of the packing and activity, while another may hide under the bed and be completely anxious. Your cat will accept the change and acclimate to her new home with understanding, love, and patience from you.

Keep the following points in mind as you prepare to move.

Packing

- Close box lids as you pack so your cat doesn't get shut into one. Boxes can be toys for a cat.
- On moving day, put your cat in an empty room and close the door so she will be safely confined while you are getting everything out of the house. Put food/water, a litter box, a bed, and a carrier in the room. Also, put something that smells like you in the room so your cat has your scent with her. Put a sign on the door instructing people to keep it closed because the family cat is in the room.

Cats Can Move, Too

At the ARL, it's always sad to see a family surrender their cat to the shelter because they are moving. If you are planning to move, make moving your cat as important as moving your children or your TV.

- Put a collar and tags (including rabies and ID) on your cat. Have your cat microchipped prior to the move.

Inside Your Car

Have the following cat supplies in your car as you move:

- A carrier, labeled with your name and contact information and emergency contact information. The carrier should have food/water, a litter box, a bed or blanket, and a shirt or towel that smells like you in it. The carrier should be large enough for your cat to stand up, turn around, and lie down comfortably.
- Plenty of water and food in case you need to refill
- Treats
- Litter and scoop
- Plastic bags for waste removal
- Bath towels or blankets to cover the carrier for additional warmth or during noisy, heavy traffic
- Paper towels and disinfecting wipes for any accidents
- Veterinarian's name and contact information and your cat's veterinary records
- Your name and contact information on the carrier, as well as an emergency contact
- Feliway® or similar spray to help keep your cat calm during transit
- Favorite toys

Reduce the Stress

Confirm early with hotels that your cat can come into the room with you. Do not leave your cat alone in the car overnight. This will add to your cat's stress. It is normal for some cats not to eat or drink very much when stressed. Monitor your cat's eating and drinking when you get to your new home. If things are not back to normal within twenty-four hours, see a veterinarian.

Cats and Collars

If your cat has never worn a collar, it is best to introduce her to it in small steps. This way, she won't see the collar as a threatening item or view it negatively. Use a breakaway collar on your cat. If the collar gets caught on something, and your cat pulls, the collar will break apart to free your cat. Cats can get caught on things outside as well as inside, so make sure you only use these types of collars.

First, let your cat sniff the collar. Put the collar on her while giving her treats. Leave the collar on for fifteen seconds. Remove the collar while petting her and giving treats.

The next day, repeat the process, this time leaving the collar on for thirty seconds. Continue the steps every day, leaving the collar on a little while longer each time until she doesn't mind it and you can leave it on all the time.

Add a tag with your name and phone number so if your cat gets lost, she can be returned to you. If you have a kitten, monitor the size of the collar as she grows to make sure that it continues to fit properly.

When You Arrive at Your New Home

Take the cat in the carrier into your new home as soon as you arrive. Place your cat in a room that no one will be going in and out of. Put the belongings she traveled with in the room with her. Close the door to the room and open the door to the carrier. Put a sign on the door that tells everyone that the cat is inside and to leave the door shut.

The first night in your new house, let your cat out to be around you after everyone else has left. Seeing you and familiar items from the old house will reduce her stress. Be sure to keep doors and windows without secure screens closed. You need to ensure that your cat does not get outside.

A Few Other Tips

These few additional tips will help make your cat's transition to a new home easier. Cats are amazingly resilient creatures, and they enjoy new places to explore and new things to discover, as long as their beloved humans are with them.

- Keep a few pieces of unwashed clothing or towels with your cat when you get to the new home. They smell like you and will give your cat comfort.
- Move your cat on the same day that you are moving. Do not take your cat to the new home one day and then move the next. Never leave your cat alone in an unfamiliar place.
- Talk to your cat in a soothing voice as you drive to your new home and are getting her set up in the new house.
- If you have more than one cat, move them all at the same time. The cats will soothe each other as they go through the moving process.
- Do not pick your cat up and force him out of the room you set up for him at the new home. Let him come out on his own.
- Do not change your cat's food.
- Do *not* let your cat outside at the new place even if she was allowed outside at the old house. She needs to learn that this is her new home and where she belongs.

↑　**Give your cat time to explore and adjust to the new home.**

When You Are Away

Some people will take their cats with them when they are away, while others make reservations at a local boarding facility. If your cat could choose, I bet she'd prefer to stay in her own home while you travel. Your cat, being a territorial creature of habit, is happy to miss out on a vacation if it means she gets to sleep in her own bed and her dinner schedule isn't interrupted.

Too many people view cats as low maintenance and choose cats as pets because of their perceived convenience. Such people may want to leave their cats alone for any length of time while they travel, but, despite what you may have heard, it's not OK to leave a cat alone with a mountain of food and a big bowl of water. Imagine the risks to your cat's health and safety, not to mention the anxiety that your cat would endure. Things can go wrong in a house with an animal left alone, such as a veterinary emergency, a fire, a flood, an electrical problem—and the list goes on. You wouldn't want your cat to suffer because no one checked on her. Additionally, it can be very stressful for a cat to find herself alone in a quiet home when she is used to the family's daily routine and interactions with her.

When planning for your cat's care while you travel, the extra precautions you take to minimize her stress and ensure her safety can be a deciding factor in whether this is a positive or negative experience for all concerned.

↑ In addition to feeding your cat, a pet sitter provides companionship and attention.

Pet Sitters

Hiring a pet sitter or having a friend or family member come over to care for your cat is a great way for you to have the security of knowing that your cat will be comfortable in her own surroundings while being safe and cared for. This can make a big difference in keeping your cat stress-free during your time away.

Do some planning when having someone else care for your cat. Don't just ask the kid next door to stop in once a day to toss some food in her bowl. You need someone who will keep your cat safe, clean the litter box, feed her, monitor her appetite and litter box use, interact with her (if your cat enjoys this), and try to minimize the stress of your absence. Hire a pet sitter who cares deeply for the welfare of his or her clients, or choose a friend or neighbor who will look out for your cat's safety, security, health, and well-being.

If your cat is used to scheduled meals, have the pet sitter come at those times to maintain the normal schedule. It can be very stressful for a cat who is used to eating two or three times a day to suddenly have to deal with only one daily meal on top of the fact that her entire family is gone. It's also not healthy for her digestion to have to eat in one meal what would usually be spread out over multiple meals.

Before You Go

A twice-daily sitter will also help ensure good litter-box hygiene and provide activity for your cat, which can make a difference in maintaining low stress levels. A visit in the morning to open the curtains and have a little playtime in addition to feeding and litter-box cleaning, followed by an evening visit to turn lights on, close the curtains, feed the cat her dinner, and have another play or petting session, can go a long way toward a calm and happy cat in your absence. The pet sitter can also leave the TV or a radio on to give the cat a sense of security.

↑ This "cat hotel" has all the amenities, but not every boarding facility is as accommodating.

Better with a Friend

If you only have one cat and are often gone overnight or on weekends, get a feline friend for your cat so that she has company. Do not get a second cat and then head out of town right away; rather, find a time when you will be home for about a month to get them acclimated to each other before you leave again. Your cat will appreciate having company while you are gone.

Boarding Facilities

There are excellent, good, average, and not-so-good boarding facilities for pets. Before you make reservations at such a facility, go there to see it yourself and take a tour. For a cat, being placed in a cage and surrounded by unfamiliar animals, sights, smells, and sounds can cause them to panic. A boarding facility with cat condos, hiding places, and elevated areas inside each cat's individual area will help your cat feel secure. Always inspect a boarding kennel from your cat's point of view and consider the following:

- How does it smell?
- How loud is the environment?
- Are the cages facing each other? (This can be very stressful.)

- Is the cage or condo big enough so that the food/water bowls are not right next to the litter box?
- How does the staff interact with the cats?
- What is done to help reduce anxiety and fear?
- Is there a veterinarian on the premises or on call for emergencies?
- How is the facility monitored at night?
- Do they offer any enrichment protocols for cats?

It's a good idea to have your cat stay for a night or two while you are still in town so you can check in with the facility to see how your cat is doing and to get your cat familiar with the facility prior to your trip.

Cat Fact

Cats spend nearly 30 percent of their time awake grooming themselves.

Grooming Your Cat
Brushing

Cats have built-in grooming brushes on their tongues, allowing them to keep themselves neat and clean. Cats will groom themselves several times a day, as they are typically fastidious animals. However, Persians and other longhaired cats need help from their owners with daily or weekly brushing sessions.

↑　Grooming time can be bonding time once your cat is used to being brushed.

↑ **Comb gently to remove any tangles.**

Start brushing your kitten at an early age so she will get used to it, and it will become a non-event. If you adopt an adult cat, start slowly with just a few brushes at a time. Gradually make the grooming sessions longer. Brushing is good for your cat's coat because it removes dirt, spreads natural oils, and prevents tangles. It can also be a great bonding activity for you and your cat.

Keep grooming sessions positive. Never raise your voice and never hold your cat down with force while you are trying to brush her. Groom your cat when you are both relaxed. Sometimes offering treats or tasty food while you are brushing is a good way for the cat to associate being groomed with a positive experience.

Here are some helpful tips:

- Touch your cat all over, including the tail, back, feet, ears, belly, and head, so she gets used to it.
- When brushing or combing, begin at your cat's head and work your way down to her tail.
- Be gentle near the chest and belly.
- Be careful around the eyes.

- If your cat has matted fur, consider taking her to a professional groomer or to your veterinarian.

Bathing

Most cats will never need a bath, but your cat will benefit from one if she gets into something smelly. If you do have to give your cat a bath, have someone help you—most cats don't like baths. Be careful when holding your cat for a bath, and talk to her in a soothing manner throughout the process. You want to minimize stress as much as you can.

To start, place something in the sink or tub for your cat to stand on so she won't slip. Next, make sure that the water is lukewarm. For adult cats, fill the sink or tub with 3 to 4 inches (7 to 10 cm) of water (less for a kitten) so she can keep most of her body out of the water.

Use a sprayer or plastic cup to thoroughly wet your cat. Be careful not get her ears, eyes, or nose wet. Using a shampoo made for cats, gently massage in the shampoo and

↑ **Your cat may never love bathtime, but she can learn to tolerate it.**

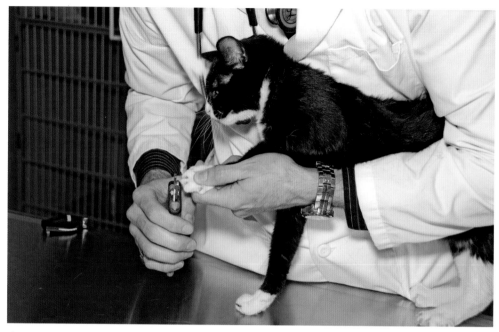

↑   Your veterinarian can clip your cat's nails during a checkup.

Polydactyl Cats

Cats normally have five toes on their front paws and four toes on their back paws. Polydactyl cats may have eight or more toes on each paw. Polydactyl cats do not suffer any health problems in relation to having extra toes, and veterinarians do not consider it a deformity or a disabling condition.

remember to keep speaking softly to your cat. Rinse with the sprayer or cup, again avoiding the eyes, ears, and nose.

After she is completely rinsed, dry your cat with a soft towel. Give her some treats after the bath to reinforce that bathtime is something positive.

Nail Clipping

- Touch your cat's feet when she is young so she is used to having her feet handled and touched. If you get a kitten, start clipping her nails early so she is used to it. Be sure to praise your cat or kitten when you touch her feet and give her treats as you are doing it. You are associating touching her paws with getting good stuff.
- Apply gentle pressure to the top of your cat's foot and the cushiony pad underneath. This will cause her to extend her claws.
- Use high-quality cat nail scissors (be sure they are sharp) to cut off the white tip of each nail, just before the point where it begins to curl.
- Be careful not to cut the "quick," a vein that runs into the nail. This pink area can be seen through the nail. If you do accidentally cut into this area, it may bleed. Apply styptic powder (available at pet-supply stores) to stop the bleeding.
- Wrap your cat in a towel, if needed, to help control her other three legs as you are trimming.
- If you are nervous about trimming your cat's nails, ask your veterinarian to do it.

Giving Pills to Your Cat

Giving your cat medicine, especially in the form of a pill, can be quite challenging. If your cat is generally cooperative in nature, you can pill her by opening her mouth and simply dropping the pill down her throat. However, most cats are not that cooperative.

Wrap your cat in a large towel so only her head protrudes. It works best to roll her in the towel and fold the end over her rear to prevent her from backing out of it. Hold the cat football-style or have her on a table facing you. Using the hand of the arm holding the cat, grasp her head by placing your hand over her head with the thumb on one side and the middle finger on the other side, just below the cheekbones. Tilt her head back until her mouth drops open slightly.

While holding her head securely in this position, grasp the pill with your other hand, using the thumb and forefinger. With the middle finger of the hand with the pill, press down on the bottom front teeth to open the mouth so you can see inside. Drop the pill in the V-shaped area at the back of her throat or place it there with your

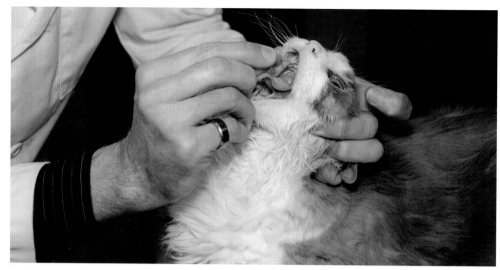

↑ Tilt the cat's head back until her mouth opens to give her a pill.

fingers. Quickly close the cat's mouth. You may want to blow gently in her face or stroke her throat to encourage swallowing. A half-dropper of diluted chicken broth or water may make it easier for your cat to swallow the pill.

Let go and watch the cat for a few moments to make sure she doesn't spit out the pill. If she spits out the pill, simply repeat the process. It may be necessary to switch to a dry pill if the initial one is sticking to your fingers. Don't throw the wet pill away, though; simply allow it to dry and administer it another time.

DID YOU KNOW?

Cats sleep approximately two-thirds of the day. This translates into sixteen hours of sleeping and eight hours of being active.

Up All Night

"My cat is keeping me awake at night" is a common complaint among pet owners. However, if you think about it, it makes sense. Cats are nocturnal, so it is normal for them to be awake and active at night.

However, this can be a problem for you when you are trying to sleep and your cat wants to play. Punishing your cat is never acceptable, especially when she is demonstrating her natural behavior.

The first question to ask yourself is, "What do I do when my cat wants my attention at night?" Do you usually get up and play with her for a while? Or do you feed her? These responses to your cat's behavior will not get you a good night's sleep. By getting up to play with your cat or give her food, you are reinforcing your cat's behavior. She gets what she wants, which results in her repeating the behavior night after night. Even if you push your cat away or tell her "no," you are still reacting to her behavior and giving her attention. You need to completely ignore your cat until the behavior stops. You must also provide toys and play with her before you go to bed.

DID YOU KNOW?

You should never allow your cat to use your bed or bedroom as a play area. Teach your cat that your bedroom is off-limits for playtime so she won't come into the bedroom to play at nighttime.

↑   Make adjustments at nighttime to keep your cat's mind off waking you up.

Adopt a Friend

Getting your cat a friend can be the solution to your nighttime-play or sleep-disruption problem; this solution has proven to be effective time and time again. The two nocturnal cats will play and keep each other company while you sleep. A second cat is also great company for your cat during the day when you are gone. Visit your local animal shelter and adopt a cat—and everyone wins.

Change Your Cat's Routine

You have two options when your cat is active at night: either switch her sleep schedule so she is sleeping at night and active during the day or give her things to occupy her at night so you can sleep. Switching your cat's sleep schedule can be difficult if you are not home during the day to tire her out by keeping her awake or playing with her.

Try playing a DVD or streaming a video that has optical appeal to cats, such as one with fish or birds moving across the screen. Watching this will keep your cat alert and interested in something other than sleep during the day. This is also a good nighttime device.

Place bird feeders outside your cat's favorite window. The birds will give your cat something other than a nap to focus on during the day.

At night, provide activities and new toys to keep your cat occupied while you are sleeping. Switch out the toys every few days so she doesn't become bored. Play with her when you get home after work and throughout the evening. This doesn't have to be several solid hours of play. Ten minutes of running after a ping-pong ball or jumping for a fishing-pole toy will seem like a long time to your cat. See chapter 7 for more information on appropriate and safe cat toys.

Shut the Door!

Q: My cat, Gus, is keeping me awake at night. I have tried shutting him out of my bedroom, but he bangs on the door, and I still can't sleep.

A: I suggested that the owner put pillows in front of the door (on the outside), making it impossible for Gus to hit the door. She called a week later and said that it had worked. Eventually, she was able to remove the pillows because Gus had gotten the message that when the door was closed, he wasn't getting in.

Hair Chewing

Q: My cat, Wally, chews on my hair while I am sleeping. How can I get him to stop?

A: Some cats like the "taste" and/or feel of hair in their mouths. Wally's owner had been pushing him away and telling him "no," but those deterrents weren't working. He kept coming back every night for more hair chewing. I explained to the owner that by pushing him away, she was still giving Wally attention, which was rewarding for him. Instead, we needed to come up with a "natural" deterrent so that her hair wasn't fun for him to chew on anymore.

I suggested that she wear a hair net or put a bad-tasting hair spray on her hair for a few nights before she went to bed. Wally would start to chew as usual, but he would then discover that he didn't like the texture, taste, or smell, and his behavior stopped.

HAPPY ENDINGS

McGee

McGee is a buff tabby that was known as Cornelius at the ARL South location. He settled in brilliantly after I adopted him. Not much was known about his history prior to coming to the ARL, except that he was a stray. When I came into the shelter, I didn't even have my heart set on taking a cat home that day. I'd been thinking about it and doing research, so I figured there was no harm in looking.

McGee laid eyes on me and never let go. He came right to me, settled into my lap, headbutted me, and purred the entire time. He essentially chose me. Honestly, what can you do when that happens?

Right from the start, McGee has provided an endless supply of affection and love. He's a *huge* cuddle monster and loves sleeping in my bed right next to me. He's not very interested in toys, but he loves his mealtimes and to be petted. He has had some small spats with the other two cats that belong to my roommate, but nothing serious. He prefers human company anyway.

—Katie

Bella

We adopted Bella from the ARL's main location. We were told that she had been surrendered by the roommate of her former owner after the owner moved out and abandoned her. We get some skeptical looks when we tell the story of how Bella chose us, but it is absolutely true. While we had her in the visiting room at the shelter, the volunteer came back to see how we were doing. I said that I really liked her, but my husband wasn't completely sold. Bella was friendly and sweet, but so quiet, and

my husband said that he likes a cat that will "talk" to you. Right at that moment, she let out a quiet little meow. We looked at each other, and then down at her in disbelief, and she meowed again! And that was when we knew it was meant to be.

These days Bella is living the life. She became good friends with our existing cat, and they really enjoy playing together. Bella spends a lot of time monitoring the bird activity from her perch on the windowsill. She plays fetch with my husband, and she loves to jump on my shoulder and ride around, rubbing her face against my cheek and purring. She fits right into our family, and we are so grateful to the ARL for bringing us together.

—Gina

Be consistent and don't give up. It may take a few days or even a few weeks, but it will be worth the effort when your cat lets you get a good night's sleep.

Cats and Christmas Trees

You can have a Christmas tree and cat at the same time with a little preparation. To start, set up the tree and leave it undecorated for a few days. If you set the tree up without decorating it, your cat can get used to it being there. Once the tree is decorated, it isn't such a new adventure.

Invest in a heavy-duty tree stand and make sure that the tree is properly and safely secured. You can add to the sturdiness of the base by attaching it to pieces of wood. When you put a tree skirt around the base of the tree, no one will see the stand.

Anchor your tree to the wall or ceiling. This is a great way to ensure that the tree doesn't topple if your cat gets curious. To do this, position the tree against a wall in front of a large picture. Remove the picture and secure the tree to the wall hook on which the picture had been hanging using fishing line and a strong hook. When you take the tree down, remove the fishing line and put the picture back.

↑ **Start by leaving the bottom of the tree undecorated.**

You can also anchor your tree by placing it under a plant hook hanging from the ceiling by a hook. Remove the plant and tie the tree to the plant hook with fishing line. After you remove the Christmas tree, put the plant back up.

Here are some helpful hints for decorating your tree:

- Initially leave the bottom third or quarter of the tree without decorations and wait a few days before adding decorations to the bottom area. The cat will have had time to adjust to the sparkling decorations before you add some within paw's reach.
- Do not use tinsel on your tree. Tinsel is very dangerous to cats, especially if swallowed.
- When you choose tree ornaments, consider types that won't be too tempting for your cat. Try to find ornaments that are heavier and don't dangle a great deal.
- Before putting the lights on your tree, coat the cords with Bitter Apple® to prevent your cat from chewing on them. (See page 124.)

↑ **This is NOT what you want to happen when you put up your Christmas tree!**

- Thread any dangling cords through PVC tubing or cable covers to further prevent your cat from chewing the cords. Paint the tubing a dark green color so it is not as noticeable against the Christmas tree.
- Use ribbon or decorative cording instead of ornament hooks to hang your ornaments. Ornament hooks can be very dangerous to cats or other pets if swallowed or chewed on. Coat the ribbon or decorative cording with Bitter Apple® so your cat won't chew them. You can then tie the ornaments securely to the tree.
- If your cat shows an interest in the tree, place a corrugated cardboard scratching post nearby. You can also grow some "kitty greens" (cat grass or catnip) and place them near the tree. If you place items like these near the tree, the cat tends to be less interested in chewing or climbing the tree and more interested in the other attractions.

Grief and Grieving Cats

Anyone who has loved and lost a pet knows the pain that comes with the loss. This is normal. Pets are a source of companionship, comfort, unconditional love, and pure joy. Many people wonder if their other pets will grieve the loss as well. The answer is yes, even though the signs may be subtle.

Grief is a reaction to the absence of something or someone who caused happiness, satisfaction, comfort, or reassurance. Cats are aware when a familiar person or companion cat is absent. They will often look for that cat or human around the house. If there are multiple cats in the home, the death or absence may change an established hierarchy. Cats may become withdrawn at the loss or maybe become clingy with their humans. If you have a cat experiencing the loss of another pet, there are some things you can do to help.

- Spend extra time playing with your cat. Pet her a little more than you usually do.
- Leave a radio or television on if your cat is home alone.
- When the time is right, adopt another pet. Choose a pet that is close in age and personality to your resident cat.
- Try not to change your cat's routine.
- In a multiple-cat home, let the surviving cats in the household work out the hierarchy on their own.

When the family structure is disrupted by the death of a person or another pet, life changes for the surviving pets. For cats, whose sense of smell is better than that of humans, this includes the absence of particular scents.

↑   **Your grieving cat may feel comforted by extra attention and cuddles.**

Your feelings may also affect your cat. Cats are sensitive to changes in human emotions, behavior, and routine. If you are upset, your cat will respond to this and may become anxious, depressed, agitated, or physically unwell. If you are finding it difficult to come to terms with your bereavement over a lost pet, you may find it helpful to talk to a pet loss hotline, your veterinarian, or someone at an animal shelter who loves animals like you do.

When there has been a human death in the family, please remember to still make time for your pets. They depend on you, and you may find comfort in them during this difficult time.

Sometimes a cat will end up at an animal shelter when her human guardian has died or gone into a care facility. This cat will be grieving the loss of her owner as well as her home and everything she knew. Adopters shouldn't expect such a cat to be playful and immediately fit into a new home and family.

Be tolerant and patient and allow the cat alone time. Keep an eye on her eating habits and physical appearance. Once your new cat has accepted you as her new caregiver, she may become clingy. Having lost one human in her life, she may not want to let you out of her sight. If you are away from home during part of the day, leave a recently worn article of clothing out so the cat can smell you.

Signs of Grief

Behavior Changes
- Changes in sleep habits
- Loss of interest in favorite activities
- Separation anxiety
- Depression
- Changes in appetite or eating patterns

Physical Changes
- Stomach upset
- Hair loss
- Overgrooming

The surviving cats will need individual attention and reassurance. If the cats were sociable, the surviving cats may search or cry out. If they were unsociable or indifferent to each other, the survivors might simply rearrange themselves into a new hierarchy, dividing up their former companion's territory between them. Sometimes the surviving cats blossom if they were previously at the bottom of the pecking order. Let the surviving cats work out the hierarchy on their own.

MEWSINGS

A Grieving Cat

Q: I had two cats, Gizmo and Shirley. Shirley passed away, and Gizmo is alone for the first time in ten years. Should I get another cat for Gizmo?

A: I talked to Gizmo's owner about the need to let him go through the grieving process of losing Shirley before deciding whether to get another cat. When cats are grieving, it is good to spend extra one-on-one time with them, especially older cats like Gizmo. Turning on a radio or TV before you go out provides some background noise and can help a grieving cat not feel so alone.

When Gizmo starts to return to normal, his owner can consider getting a second cat. For Gizmo, an older cat is definitely the way to go. Both cats will want to do the same types of activities.

Alternatively, she may remain aloof. Don't press attention on an unwilling cat, but do spend time in the same room and talk to her. Encourage her to interact with you. The settling-in process may take longer, so be patient.

Myths About Cats

Here are some real answers about common myths surrounding cats to dispel any misinformation that may be circulating.

Myth: Black cats are bad luck.
Truth: In Japan, black cats are considered good luck.

Myth: Cats always land on their feet.
Truth: Cats do instinctively fall feet first, but they may also break bones and incur other injuries.

Myth: Cats should drink milk every day.
Truth: People tend to believe that cats love milk and need milk in their diets. It is true that they tend to like milk, but they do not need it for proper nourishment. We suggest that you do not give your cat milk at all.

Myth: Cats get their balance from their whiskers.
Truth: Cats use their whiskers to feel, not for balance.

Myth: If you are pregnant, you need to get rid of your cat.
Truth: Sadly, hundreds of cats are relinquished to animal shelters every year because of this myth. It is true that some cats can be infected with a disease called *toxoplasmosis*, which occasionally can be spread to humans through litter boxes and cause serious problems in unborn babies. However, these risks can be controlled if the expectant mother avoids contact with the litter box and assigns daily cleaning to a friend or other family member. Personal hygiene, such as frequent hand washing, is another important factor in preventing transmission. If you are concerned, talk with your doctor.

Myth: Cats may try to suffocate babies.
Truth: A cat may try to get into a crib with a baby because the baby is new or warm or smells good. But there is no intent on the part of the cat to suffocate or "steal the breath" from a baby. (See Cats and Babies on page 170.)

Myth: Cats are aloof.
Truth: Cats can tend to be aloof and more standoffish at first, but they will absolutely bond with their caretakers and, ultimately, their owners.

Myth: If a cat is injured, she can lick her wounds, and the wounds will heal automatically from the saliva.
Truth: Actually, licking can slow the healing process and cause further issues. If your cat is injured, she needs to see a veterinarian.

Myth: Cats are unhappy if they are kept indoors.
Truth: For a cat that is used to being outside, there may be an adjustment period when keeping her inside all of the time, but it can be done. It's important to never let her outside again. Give her access to windows to look out, and provide her with plenty of toys and companionship inside the house. Inside cats live much longer and healthier lives than outside cats. (See Chapter 14.)

↑　**Cats like milk, but we do not recommend giving it to your cat.**

Myth: Cats don't really like people and don't need a lot of care.

Truth: Cats may appear to be independent in nature, but cats are social creatures and require care just like any other pets. Cats tend to live longer because of the level of care we are able to provide for them. More cats are being treated like members of the family and forming strong bonds with their humans.

Myth: All female cats should have a litter of kittens before being spayed.

Truth: Spaying a cat will help prevent such issues as mammary cancer, ovarian cysts, and pregnancy complications, including stillbirth and malformed kittens. There is no medical or behaviorial reason your cat should have a litter of kittens before being spayed. The reality is that some people just don't want to spend the money to have their cats spayed, so they sometimes make excuses to avoid doing it. Cat overpopulation in the United States is out of control and unacceptable. It is important to spay or neuter your cat.

Myth: Cats and dogs hate each other.

Truth: Unfortunately, the entertainment industry has helped to perpetuate this myth. The reality is that cats are totally capable of affectionate and close relationships with dogs. Pets form relationships with other pets, and they seem to understand that they are all part of the family.

MEWSINGS

Water-Bowl Issues

Q: My cat, Jack, splashes water out of his water dish and all over the floor. I am tired of constantly cleaning up the mess.

A: Some cats think that this is a fun game. You can put out multiple bowls with just a little water in each so that Jack won't have a big pool to play in. You can also put a few rocks in the bottom of the water bowl before adding water. Jack may not like the look of the bottom of the bowl as much without a reflection to play in.

Chewing Furniture

Q: My cat, Max, is a year old and recently started chewing on a leather chair. How can I get him to stop doing this?

A: I suggested that Max's owner take Max to the vet to make sure there was not a food issue as well as to spray the chair with a pet-safe bitter substance that would not harm the leather. Max will likely decide that the chair isn't fun anymore and will stop chewing. I also recommended that the owner give Max some new toys with different textures to chew on.

Toilet Paper

Q: My two adult female cats have discovered the toilet paper roll. They have decided it's fun to unroll the entire thing while I sleep.

A: First, either shut the bathroom door at night or remove the toilet paper roll at night for a week or so. The cats will become bored and will seek other playthings. Supplement with a variety of toys.

Free-Feeding

Q: I have three indoor cats, all around four years old, and I feed them once in the morning and once at night in a central location. All of them occasionally vomit after they eat, and I'm worried. There doesn't seem to be a medical reason for this.

A: I talked to the owner about free-feeding; that is, leaving dry food out for the cats all the time so they can eat when they want. We also talked about setting up different feeding locations around the house. Because all three cats were hungry in the morning, and they had a set amount of food in one location, they would eat quickly without chewing or digesting properly, causing them to vomit.

The cats' owner set up three feeding locations and started leaving food out for them at all times. After a while, the cats realized that there would always be food available, and the vomiting stopped.

Lelu

Living in the country, we are regularly visited by cats, kittens, dogs, and puppies. While the adult animals may be strays, we think that the kittens and puppies are dumped and abandoned. Lelu is one of the lucky kittens. She found her way to our home one summer night. We heard the mewing and went outside to see a small, skinny, scared kitten of about four months old. She was very fearful. She was also very hungry. She had no interest in coming close to strangers, and we didn't know whether or not she was feral.

Each night, we brought food to our garage to entice her inside and give her safe shelter. After about a week, we offered the food in our hands, hoping she'd come close. It took some time, but she did eventually allow us to touch her, and about a week after that, she allowed us to pet her.

We set up a litter box in the garage that she started using right away. She became more confident and sociable. After getting a clean bill of health from our vet, we put out the word that this pretty kitten needed a forever home. Michelle adopted lucky little Lelu. She now thrives happily in a family with three rescued cats and two rescued dogs.

—Jeramy

Callie

My cat's name is Callie, and I adopted her from the ARL main location. She was a little calico bundle of joy, and she immediately won over every member of my family. Because we had such a great success with Callie, my family adopted all of their future pets from the

ARL. It was also because of Callie that I started volunteering at the ARL and have continued to do so. I enjoy helping people adopt pets that will bring them as much happiness as Callie has brought to me.

Callie's life now is pretty *purr*-fect. She is a spoiled only child who is spending her senior years in the West Des Moines area and enjoys spending time outside in her "catio." Callie truly means the world to me. She is so sweet and is always by my side. She brings so much happiness to my life. Thank you, ARL, for helping me and others have these great success stories with such wonderful pets.

—Meghan

HAPPY ENDINGS

Maude

I was at the ARL, cleaning with the usual volunteer group that cleans every holiday so the staff can have time off to be with their families. It happened to be Easter, and I met a cat named Maude. She was an eight-year-old stray waiting to go up for adoption. Maude and I had an instant connection that day. I couldn't get her out of my mind, and I visited her every time I was at the shelter after that.

I cleaned again on the Fourth of July, and Maude was still there, waiting for a home. After finishing the cleaning and feeding, I was walking away from her to go home, and I had a feeling that she was looking at me. I turned around to look over my shoulder at her. She was squeezed and leaning toward the front of her cage just so she could watch me walk away. I went back and opened her cage. She headbutted me, and I whispered in her ear that I would be back for her.

I drove home that day and started thinking about all of the wonderful cats, like Maude, that had been at the ARL for so long, waiting for homes, and the idea for a Summer Cat Getaway program came to me. The first cat in the program was Maude. I thought that, at a minimum, I could get her out of her cage and find her a temporary home with one of my friends. Instead, she came to my house, and my husband, Tom, and I ended up adopting her. It just shows what a bond between a person and a cat can do.

The Summer Cat Getaway program is still going strong and has helped find homes for a majority of the cats in the program. Maude will never know what she accomplished!

—Carol

18 Closing Thoughts

All of us who love our own cats also need to help other cats. Animal shelters across the country take in millions of cats, and they all need second chances and homes.

The ARL takes in more than 20,000 animals in a given year. Typically, more than half of them are cats and kittens. It is our responsibility to do what we can to help.

Spay/Neuter

Spay or neuter your own cats and kittens, whether they go outside or not. One slip out the door for an unaltered cat can cause a pregnancy. If you hear a coworker, friend, or family member talking about his or her cats, ask if the cats are altered. If they aren't, help get the cats spayed or neutered, even if you have to pay to have it done. Make spaying and neutering a priority for you and other cat owners.

Educate

Educate your friends about the cat overpopulation problem. Make sure that your friends know what is happening in the United States with cat overpopulation. Get them engaged in helping to spread the word. Typically, people don't want to hear sad stories, but the overpopulation problem *is* sad, and people need to hear about it so we can work together to solve it.

Adopt

If you are looking for a cat or kitten, adopt one from a shelter. There are wonderful cats of every age, breed, color, personality, and sex in every animal shelter in this country. Save a life. Adopt. Even better—adopt two!

Volunteer

Donate your time, whether it is one hour a week or one day a week, and volunteer at a local animal shelter. Work at an event, clean cages, socialize cats, help with adoptions—just volunteer and make a difference. People say they "can't" volunteer because it makes them sad to see animals in need of homes, but the cats need you! The cats and kittens at shelters are in safe places with food, shelter, and love, and you can help them find forever homes.

Be Active

Be aware of, involved with, and active in animal protection legislation. For

Shelter Cats Need *You*

For more than twenty years, I have spent time in animal-shelter work. I have seen things and heard things that I wish I had not, but, at the same time, those things have had a profound effect on me. Every day at an animal shelter is a challenge, but I have always gotten more than I have given in one way or another. Get involved and help. The cats are counting on you.

example, if your community doesn't have mandatory spay/neuter laws, research the legislative process and see what you can do to get these laws introduced and passed.

Donate

Donate money to your local animal shelter. Shelters love the animals they care for, and it costs money to feed them and provide them with veterinary care. Donate whatever you can; it all makes a difference.

Go Home and Hug Your Cat

At the end of the workday, go home and hug your cat. Make a commitment to your cat that you will always care for her. Make arrangements with a trusted family member or friend so if something happens to you, he or she will take your cat and care for her; put these arrangements in writing. Your state may even allow you to set up a pet trust.

HAPPY ENDINGS

Sophie and Titus

I adopted Titus and Sophie (Shelby) from the ARL main location about a month after my cat of fifteen years died. It was such a hard loss that I had decided I didn't want any more cats. My niece eventually talked me in to going to the ARL just to look, and, after several trips, we saw this cute little kitten, but he was hardly ever in his cage. When one of the volunteers came and asked us if we needed help, we told her we wanted to see him but he must be popular because he kept

disappearing. She told us that was because he was very interactive and would cry until someone took him out to play with him. When we got to meet him, we fell in love.

That night, I went on the ARL website, knowing that I would eventually adopt a second cat so that the kitten would have a playmate, and I found Miss Sophie. I met her the next day, and she was just as sweet as the shelter volunteers had described. Both the kitten and Sophie had been found as strays, and the volunteers weren't sure if either of them had been around other cats. We were concerned that one-year-old Sophie, being on the shy side, might not be too sure about an ornery little four-month-old boy, but we decided to give it a try.

I brought the kitten (Titus) and Sophie home that night, and once they had thoroughly checked out their new digs, they started to play together—and they have been best buddies ever since. They are so good together. I've never heard either of them hiss at the other. When they lie down near each other, one of them usually has an outstretched paw, touching the other one.

Titus is still the ornery little boy we met at the shelter. If there is unattended food anywhere near him, watch out! And when we come in from outside and I take off his harness, he cries at the back door and puts his paws on the handle to try to open it. He is just a curious little boy that watches everything I do.

Sophie is the same little sweetheart as when I first brought her home. I discovered early on that she likes to give nose kisses. I saw her on several occasions touch noses with Titus, so I made a kissing sound and she came right over and touched her nose to mine. She curls up next to me on the couch at night and gently works my hand around until she can get my thumb in her mouth to suck on it.

I have never had any animals quite like these two. They are both so sweet and loving and full of personality. They put a smile on my face daily and I'm so grateful that my niece talked me in to going to the ARL after my loss, because I can't imagine life without them!

—Laurie

HAPPY ENDINGS

Snowball

Ever since I was a little girl, I have loved cats. Unfortunately, it was the one animal my parents would not allow me to have because I was extremely allergic. Even so, every Christmas, I would ask for a cat.

When I was eight, I specifically asked for a fluffy white cat with blue eyes named Snowball. That Christmas, I got a stuffed fluffy white cat with blue eyes; of course, I named her Snowball.

After I graduated from high school and got my first apartment, I was determined to adopt a cat, despite my allergies. Spanky, a gray domestic shorthair kitten, became my new roommate. As it turned out, I had actually outgrown my allergy to cats, so I soon adopted another cat, a Maine Coon named Capone.

Over the next several years, I adopted three large dogs, bringing the total number of animals in my house to five. I decided I was at my limit for animals. One morning, however, I walked into the ARL and saw a litter of kittens. There, among several other kittens, was a fluffy white cat with blue eyes. I do not even remember what the shelter had named her, because from the moment I saw her, I thought, *Snowball*!

Already at my self-imposed "animal limit," I had absolutely zero intention of adopting another animal, so when I saw that the kitten already had two adoption applications, I was a little relieved. But throughout the rest of the day, I could not get her out of my head. Twenty years after getting my stuffed Snowball, I saw the cat I had always envisioned.

I couldn't fight fate, so the next day I decided I would apply to adopt her and be third in line. If it worked out, it was meant to be; if not, she would still have a great home with someone else. Well, it was meant to be. The first applicant called and changed her mind, and the second never showed up. The potential adopters' deadline to adopt her was at noon that day, so at 12:01 p.m., I was completing the adoption contract to bring Snowball home.

Snowball taught me that you cannot always choose the pets you are destined to be with, and despite my "limit," there was still room in my heart and my home for one more. Snowball's story was twenty years in the making, and now I look forward to spending the next twenty years living with her instead of just dreaming of her.

—Stephanie (text and photo reprinted with permission, *dsm Magazine*)

Index

Publisher's Acknowledgments

The publisher wishes to acknowledge and thank the many people who tirelessly and with great compassion care for shelter animals and especially those who worked to make this book happen.

Thank you to Carol Griglione, who, drawing on her more than two decades of experience specifically focused on cats, cat issues, and cat behaviors, spent countless hours developing this book and making sure that the advice and guidance given here is what cat owners most need to know to live successfully with their rescue cats.

Thank you to Mick McAuliffe. In addition to managing the ARL's shelter operations and training and counseling pet owners on pet behavior issues, Mick was there whenever he was needed to help in preparing and reviewing this book.

Special thanks to Tom Colvin, whose vision and dedication, along with Carol's, created the state-of-the-art animal shelter that is the Animal Rescue League of Iowa.

Thank you to all of the following people for their dedication to shelter animals and help with this book: Dr. Dan Campbell, Chief Staff Veterinarian, ARL-Iowa Main Shelter; Stephanie Filer, Manager Special Gifts and Partnerships, ARL-Iowa; the entire ARL-Iowa staff; the owners who contributed the rescue stories and photos for this book; Carol McGarvey, contributing editor; Dr. Kersti Seksel, Registered Veterinary Specialist, Behavioral Medicine, and Dr. Gaille Perry, Veterinary Behaviorist, Sydney Animal Behaviour Service; Dr. Amy Marder, VMD, Certified Applied Animal Behaviorist; Dr. Amanda Gigler, Co-Owner/Medical Director, Ankeny Animal and Avian Clinic.

Thank you to the following invaluable resources: Animal Rescue League of Iowa (*www.arl-iowa.org*); Humane Society of the United States (*www.humanesociety.org*); The American Society for the Prevention of Cruelty to Animals (*www.aspca.org*); American Humane Association (*www.americanhumane.org*); Animal Veterinary Medical Association (*www.avma.org*); Alley Cat Allies, Trap-Neuter-Return Program for feral cats (*www.alleycat.org*).

Photo Credits

Front cover and title page: Shutterstock/PHOTOCREO Michal Bednarek

Back cover: Shutterstock/Svetlana Popov (top); Gladkova Svetlana (bottom)

Pawprint graphic, cover and page 3: Shutterstock/Zsschreiner

Chapter opener/sidebar background, pages 1–6, 9–11, 16, 18–19, 25–27, 32–33, 44–47, 54–55, 69–72, 74–75, 83–85, 88, 90, 92–93, 100, 102–103, 110–113, 119–121, 127–129, 138–139, 154–155, 162–163, 170–171, 195, 204–205, 208–209, 212–215, 223–224 : Shutterstock/wow.subtropica

"Happy Endings" graphic, pages 9, 45, 127, 153, 213: Shutterstock/Nampueng

"Mewsings" graphic, pages 15, 70, 72–73, 78, 82, 90–91, 100, 119, 149, 161, 195, 201, 204–205: Shutterstock/Julia Kutanina

Courtesy Kelly Kesling, Kesling Photography: 6, 223, 224

Courtesy Animal Rescue League of Iowa: 4, 7–9, 22, 23 (top), 24, 29, 34, 37 (top), 44, 45, 50, 53, 58 (bottom), 59 (top), 73, 76, 83, 95 (top), 97, 101, 110, 111, 115 (top), 127, 146, 149, 153, 169, 172, 181, 190 (top), 191, 196, 197, 206, 207, 212–214

Courtesy Shutterstock: 135pixels, 189; 4 PM production, 47; 5 second Studio, 88 (top); absolutimages, 60 (top), 64–65 (bottom), 70; Africa Studio, 12, 23 (bottom), 40, 66–67, 71, 91, 95 (bottom), 119, 173, 178, 182, 195; ajlatan, 65 (top); Poprotskiy Alexey, 41 (top); Alexlukin, 123; amstockphoto, 143; Anna Andersson Fotografi, 117; aprilante, 171; Aspen Photo, 30; Ermolaev Alexander, 13 (bottom); Nikolay Bassov, 118; Beautiful landscape, 150; Andriy Blokhin, 130, 136, 155; Helen Bloom, 103; bmf-foto.de, 133; Xeniya Butenko, 186; Tony Campbell, 89 (bottom); Martin Carlsson, 107; Jaromir Chalabala, 90, 184; Chereliss, 88 (bottom graphic); chromatos, 104; Osaze Cuomo, 113; cynoclub, 160, 179; De Jongh Photography, 106 (bottom); Esin Deniz, 114; donikz, 25; Vikentiy Elizarov, 77 (bottom); encierro, 20, 115 (bottom); Evdoha_spb, 96, 166; evrymmnt, 167; Bussakorn Ewesakul, 183; GaevoyB, 109; Gumpanat, 106 (top); Martin Hass, 193; Steve Heap, 140; Vika Hova, 87; Impact Photography, 13 (top); Eric Isselee, 105, 108 (bottom), 156 (bottom); IvoryNS, 121; Jagodka, 17; JakubD, 93, 125 (bottom); KARNSTOCKS, 57 (top); a katz, 19; KOKTARO, 108 (top); Ekatsyerina Kostsina, 63; Ingus Kruklitis, 126; Andrey_Kuzmin, 58 (top), 88 (center); Kzenon, 156 (top); Lapina, 28, 176; Fernanda Leite, 159; Helen Liam, 69; LightField Studios, 52; Lightspruch, 55; Tanya Little, 78; Anatoliy Lukich, 145; Lux Blue, 190 (bottom); Dorottya Mathe, 41 (bottom); Melissa Sue, 122; Muk, 116; MW47, 198; Mylimages – Micha; DenisNata, 131; Chirtsova Natalia, 31; New Africa, 56, 62; noreefly, 98; Pelagey, 89 (top); Kseniia Perminova, 27; Photo Melon, 125 (top); Playa del Carmen, 68; Svetlana Popov, 79; OFC Pictures, 15; Okssi, 11; Olga_DigitalWork, 59 (bottom); Sari ONeal, 42; otsphoto, 144; Taya Ovod, 165; Alena Ozerova, 36, 38, 99, 174; photosounds, 16; ANURAK PONGPATIMET, 134 (bottom), 187; PorChonlawit, 85; PRESSLAB, 49; Rappholdt, 129; RJ22, 94, 177; SariMe, 141; t-schankz, 134 (top); South O Boy, 151; SpeedKingz, 175; Susan Schmitz, 33, 194; Benjamin Simeneta, 77 (top); sunfun, 86 (bottom); Suphaksorn Thongwongboot, 163; topseller, 147; Oleg Troino, 157; Tsekhmister, 37 (bottom); Tuzemka, 86 (top), 158; AttilaVarga, 135; Elya Vatel, 75; Sonsedska Yuliia, 14; StockPhotosArt, 57 (bottom); Studio Ayutaka, 215; Sydneymills, 35; Veera, 199; Joyce Vincent, 164; vvita, 152; Sergey Yaskevich, 142; Bahadir Yeniceri, 192; Jakub Zak, 188; Dora Zett, 60 (bottom), 124, 132, 161, 185; Stephanie Zieber, 137

About the Authors

Carol Griglione has worked on a wide range of animal issues in Iowa for close to three decades, including those issues affecting animal shelters. She has been involved in such areas as making animal torture and dog fighting a felony in Iowa, and she has focused specifically on cats for more than twenty years. She is chair of the board of directors of the ARL; sits on the board of the Iowa Federation of Humane Societies; and regularly speaks on topics related to cat behavior.

Carol holds a bachelor's degree in communications from Simpson College in Indianola, Iowa, and a master's degree in nonprofit management from Drake University in Des Moines. She started volunteering with the Animal Rescue League of Iowa in the early 1990s and threw herself into study, attending conferences and seminars around the United States, learning from other behavior experts. Carol coordinates the ARL's Catsnip Spay/Neuter Program and Summer Cat Getaway Program. Carol credits her first cat, Azzurro, with her passion for understanding cats and their behavior and for helping people learn about them to keep them in their homes and out of shelters. A native Iowan, Carol resides in Runnells with her husband and their three dogs, seven cats, three horses, and twelve pet chickens.

Mick McAuliffe joined the ARL's staff in November 2009 as the Pet Behavior and Enrichment Manager and currently serves as Director of Animal Services. Before coming to the United States, Mick served as the Director of Animal Behavior and Training for the RSPCA Queensland, Australia, where he developed assessment, modification, and training programs for multiple species. In addition to his extensive work in canine training, Mick has applied his training skills to a variety of animals, from Sea World Australia's large marine mammals to a collection of 130 native and exotic birds, developing free-flight shows for visitors. He has lectured on animal behavior across five continents, working extensively in Australia, Japan, China, England, Saudi Arabia, and the United States.

Mick believes that pets live with us as part of our family, learning what we like and dislike through everyday life experiences rather than through strict leadership and training. He teaches using only positive-reinforcement techniques, eliminating the need for physical or verbal correction or training equipment that can cause pain or injury. He educates owners on how to teach their pets with patience and understanding, resulting in well-mannered pets and lifelong bonds. Mick and his wife, Caitlin, share their home with four cats; their dog, Lucy; and their birds, Jack and Zane. All are rescues.